THE CONFEDERATE MILITARY COMMISSION HELD IN SAN ANTONIO, TEXAS

July 2—October 10, 1862
As Pertains To The
Insurgency Resulting in The
Nueces Battle

Compiled and Edited

By

Wm. Paul Burrier, Sr.

Watercress Press
San Antonio, 2014

A *Watercress Press* book
from Geron & Associates
www. watercresspress.com

ISBN-13: 978-0934955-06-5
LC #2014934040

Cover image by Wm. Paul Burrier, Sr.
Cover design by 3iii's Graphic Studios

Contents

Introduction 1

Confederate States vs. Joseph Krust 5

Confederate States vs. Leonhard Peterick 6

Confederate States vs. Julius Schlickum 7

Confederate States vs. Valentine Haass 16

Confederate States vs. Philip Braubach 17

Confederate States vs. Frederick Lochte 38

Confederate States vs. J. R. Radcliff 43

Confederate States vs. H. J. Richarz 53

Confederate States vs. Blasins Kieffer 54

Confederate States vs. Joseph Wipff 55

Confederate States vs. Eduard Degener 56

Confederate States vs. Ferdinand Simon 94

ENDNOTES 99

Introduction

A large number of Germans settled the Texas Hill Country in the late 1840s and early 1850s. Most of these were farmers, stone masons, craftsmen, and so forth. With the group was a small number of Freethinkers. After the failed 1848-49 German Revolution several hundreds of the radical leaders joined the earlier Germans in the Hill Country. These Forty-Eights joined with the Freethinkers and attempted to organize a German politically party. One of their goals was to establish a free state in Western Texas [Now the Texas Hill Country]. It was only at the start of the Civil War did they see a real chance to do so. They organized an insurgency. In June 1861 the political element was created. Today this political element is called the Union Loyal League, but the insurgents similarly called it 'the organization'. The insurgents believed that the Union was going to invade Texas with two prongs. One invasion force would land at Galveston. The second would drive overland from Kansas. These two prongs would linkup at Austin splitting the state in two along the Colorado River. It was the area west of the Colorado that the Free State of West Texas would be organized. In March 1862 the insurgents organized the military element of the insurgency. It was battalion size with somewhere between 300 and 500 members. This battalion was a secret unauthorized military unit solely devoted to the creation of West Texas. When the Union invasion came, this battalion would rise up and with armed Unionist units in Austin, San Antonio, and Bandera, Comal and Medina Counties would declare The Free State of West

Texas. Meantime the insurgents would remain members of the local militia units. All white males in Texas above the age of 18 and under 45 were required to be a member of a militia unit.

Bandera County had a Unionist company of about 45 members and Medina had Unionist control of a battalion of four companies with about 350 members.

The insurgent battalion began to organize and conduct guerrilla operations which culminated with the death of at least two secessionists. The Confederate Military Commander of Texas declared Martial Law over the entire state and sent regular Confederate units into the Hill Country to destroy the insurgency. With the arrival of regular Confederate troops the hard-core of the insurgency, sixty-three in number, decided to flee Texas, go to Mexico, and on to New Orleans and join the Union Army. All of the insurgent forces were deserters from either their militia units or the Confederate Army.

A hundred-man pursuit force overtook the insurgents on August 10, 1862 on the West Prong of the Nueces River. What occurred next was a hard-fought battle. The Confederates assaulted the insurgency camp three times and were forced back. Twenty-eight of the insurgents gave up the fight and left their comrades. Therefore on the fourth assault the Confederates captured the insurgent camp. A total of nineteen insurgents were killed at the battle site to include about seven wounded who were executed. The Confederates lost six men killed or died from their wounds and fifteen men wounded, of which at east five received medical discharges.

Introduction

A number of insurgency leaders and Unionist sympathizers were arrested and tried before a Confederate Military Commission held in San Antonio from July 2 and October 10, 1862. This is the account of those tried before the Military Commission who were involved in the insurgency or resistance movement.

July 17, 1862
Confederate States[1] vs. Joseph Krust[2]

This case coming on for trial and the Commission being satisfied that the prosecution has entirely failed, and that it was set on foot *(sic)* through malice, the party was discharged from custody.

July 17, 1862
Confederate States[3] vs. [Leonhard] Peterick[4]

This case coming on for trial, the prisoner was brought before the Commission and being interrogated, said that he was 37 years of age and was born in Hanover, Germany. Was charged with depreciating the currency and disloyalty; but the charge not being sufficiently sustained and the accused, [Leonhard] Peterick, expressing a willingness to go into service of the Confederate States, was duly sworn in by the Judge Advocate and was turned over to Captain S. G. Newton,[5] Commanding Post of San Antonio.

July 17, 1862
Confederate States[6] vs. Julius Schlickum[7]

Erastus Reed[8] [sworn] says:

I have known Mr. Schlickum about one year. Judging from his conversations I don't think he has any sympathy for the Confederate States. I know of no act that he has ever done against the Government, his general conversations has been such as would lead anyone to suppose that he was opposed to the Confederacy. [He] knows of nothing particular except his manner of expression at the reception of the news.

He [accused] never appeared to believe anything coming from the Confederates, but on the contrary would always credit the news from our enemies. His associates generally were those who were looked upon with suspicion. He always appeared to know a great deal of those who were looked upon with suspicion. He once told me that he did not believe that Radeleff[9] and Doebbler[10] were any more disloyal than he was. He said he asked Radcliff and Doebbler if they belonged to that organization, to which they answered in the negative. The Accused said he knew of such an organization, but that it was for self defense. He said he knew there were over one hundred men out in the woods, said he did not belong to the organization.[11] About the time Duff's Company was there the Prisoner asked me whether he would be arrested, said rather than be arrested he would have to go into the woods. He finally said that he done nothing and would not go.

He also told me that there was an organization in San Antonio.[12] He said that he believed they were mostly boys and they could be easily put down. He believed he knew men who belonged to it. He assured me that he did not belong to such an organization. I have never known him to construe any news favorable to the Confederacy.

By the Defendant:

I never saw the accused associate with anyone looked upon with suspicion, except persons who came to the Defendant's store. Do you recollect after a singing festivity in Boerne, I told you as follows—Doebbler and Radcliff were passing through Boerne from San Antonio. I told Mr. Reed that rumors were floating about our vicinity that secret organizations were up in the mountains? Answer. So you told me and told me that he believed that Judge Scott[13] and men like him had started such organizations by threatening the lives of those who did not believe as they did about Political matters and that it was for self defense.

I remember the accused told me he had had a conversation with Radeleff and Doebbler about such an organization, and that he, "the accused," had told Radcliff and Doebbler that he did not believe they were such fools, as to be guilty of joining such an organization, which would only bring destruction on the people and bloodshed on the frontier. I know he told me that there was such an organization in San Antonio. I think [John] Holzappel[14] was present when this conversation took place. The whole neighborhood frequented his store. Judge Scott is an Ultra Southern man.

Signed
Erastus Reed

George Wilkins Kendall[15] a witness, was then called before the Commission and being duly sworn deposed as follows:

I live in four or five miles of the accused. I never heard the accused say anything by which I could judge whether he was in favor of one Government or the other. I know nothing of the accused opinions on the Slavery question. I never heard anyone say that the accused was a friend to the South. I never asked anyone whether the accused was friendly to the South.

Signed
George Wilkins Kendall

Erastus Reed was then recalled before the Commission and being duly sworn, deposed as follows:

I have hear the accused say that he was born in Europe and was in favor of free labor and opposed to the institution of slavery. He told me this in his own store. I don't remember who was present. I cannot say what brought on the conversation, it was sometime ago. I took it that this referred to Slavery in Texas. I think anyone entertaining such views is an Abolitionist and would be in favor of abolishing Slavery.

Signed
Erastus Reed

Joseph Graham[16] was then called before the Commission and being sworn deposed as follows:

I live three miles from Boerne. I make my visits to town as short as possible. I sometimes called at the store of the accused, he always appeared to be in possession of news, more favorable to the North than to the South. I have never heard him express his opinion on the justice or injustice of the war. When Captain Duff's Company was up the country the accused told me that he heard he was to be arrested, asked my advice as what he should do.

He said that if it depended on Captain Duff he would go and report himself but that he might have orders to arrest him. He said he might have sung some Yankee songs, but that he was drunk, and did not think it treason. I told the accused that he was accused of being an Abolitionist. He said, "I was brought up in Europe and my views and yours differ."

He did not say that he was opposed to the institution here, but remarked as above. I have never been intimate with the accused. I have not heard accused spoken of, as regards Abolitionism, more than the generality of Germans. I know the accused was opposed to Secession and I have seen nothing since to induce me to think he had changed his views.

Accused knew that I was one of four or five out of an hundred who voted for Secession, and when I was a Candidate for Chief Justice he did more for me than I did for myself.

Signed
Joseph Graham

10

* * *

July 18, 1862

The Case of Julius Schlickum coming up the accused was brought before the Commission.

Seamen Field[17] 1st sergeant in Duff's Company T.P.D. being duly sworn and deposed as follows:

I know of nothing particular against the accused, but have always supposed him to be against us. He was not in the habit of presenting our successes in a fair light. I mean by that, that he never had any good news on our side, but generally had something bad to tell. I have regarded him as being dangerous, from the fact, that those to whom he would communicate his news were governed by what he would say. I know of no open acts, further than as stated, except depreciating Confederate Currency. I know of his being opposed to taking Confederate currency and advised others not to do so. This was previous to the proclamation establishing Martial law. I have lived in four miles, of the accused for two years, except the last three months. I know the general reputation of accused in his section, as regards his loyalty of this Government, and it is bad. Accused is a man of considerable influence in his section, he is a merchant, he is a man of more than ordinary intelligence, or more than the majority of the people he lives with. He informs himself of transpiring events.

By the Accused.

I heard about the month of February last, that accused refused to take Confederate Money. I have heard you advise people not to take Confederate Money. Accused advised me not to take it. He told me if I had any, I had better get shut *(sic)* of it, as it would be worth nothing in a short time.

That the U. S. Army was getting the best of us and we would be whipped soon and the money would be worthless. I have seen accused associated with no suspicious character, except countrymen of accused who I regarded as being influenced by accuser's advice. Slasson was constantly about the accuser's Store, and I regarded him as a very suspicious and dangerous character.

Signed
Seamen Field

* * *

July 19, 1862

The Prisoner Julius Schlickum was brought before the Commission and presented the following defense.

To the Honorable Military Commission San Antonio
Gentlemen,

In conformity with your desire, I submit to you in the following my defense against the accusations brought against me. My charges couched in such general terms that I concluded to call three gentlemen as witnesses, or rather references who were known as good and loyal Citizens, though I was not so well acquainted with them, that they could give other than general evidence.

These gentlemen all state, that I have often communicated news, unfavorable to the South, but Colonel Graham admits, that, at the time, there was no other news to communicate I do not deny, that, in some instances, I have doubted the reports of News Papers, which, I believe everybody did, more or less.

Mr. Reed says, that he had often seen me in company with people, who were looked upon with suspicion, but he was forced to admit, never outside my store. I am a merchant and have no business with my customer's politics, how Mr. Reed can make this out to be a crime, as it appears to be his intention, is more than malicious.

A similar malice is contained in the repetition of a conversation, which I had sometime ago with this gentlemen, about a secret society, which was said to have organized in the mountains. He said at first that I had said, I *know* of such association, but on being cross questioned, was forced to admit, that I had only talked about *floating rumors*.

Mr. Reed says further, that I had talked about a similarly society in San Antonio, but could not produce the witness who he said, had been present. I most emphatically deny ever having said such things and consider my *No!* to be entitled to just as much credence as Mr. Reed's *Yes!*

The testimony of the three gentlemen is clear, I do not consider it necessary, to say much about it; but the Colonel Graham, the only one of my accusers, who voted for Secession has treated me more favorable in his evidence, than the other two gentlemen, who formerly held the same political opinion with me. Do they try, by accusing me, to make their antecedents forgotten?

I have always obeyed the laws of the land, have taken the oath, prescribed by law, and committed no illegal act, and I am willing to do my duty as a citizen of these Confederate States. May the Court take into consideration, that I am a man of small means, have a large family, and that my wife is continually ailing and that from your decision, the welfare, nay, the existence of a whole family is depending.

Hoping soon to receive a judgment, which will enable me to return to my family.

I remain
Gentlemen
Your Obedient Servant
Julius Schlickum

* * *

July 25, 1862

The defendant Julius Schlickum is charged with being a disloyal person to the Confederate States of America. That in his general deportment he is calculated to create dis-content, and dissatisfaction, with this Government and its currency.

Confederate States vs. Julius Schlickum

Signed
John Ireland
Judge Advocate and Recorder

The statement of parties being thus in possession of the Commission, the Commission was cleared for deliberation and having maturely considered the evidence adduced, fined the accused Julius Schlickum, Guilty of Charge and Specification.

And the Commission does thereby sentence the said Julius Schlickum to be "Imprisoned until peace is ratified between the United States and the Confederate State."

July 18, 1862
Confederate States[18] vs. V [Valentine] Haass[19]

This case coming on for trial, the accused was brought before the Commission and being interrogated, responded as follows:

I am 34 years of age, born in Germany and am perfectly willing to go into the Army of the Southern Confederacy. There being no charges alleged, the accused was sworn into the army of the Confederate States, by the Judge Advocate and was turned over to Captain S. G. Newton, Commanding Post at San Antonio.[20]

July 22, 1862
Confederate States[21] vs. Philip Braubach[22]

Mr. Wolman [Michael Vollmer[23]] being sworn says:

About 3 months since I heard accused say that the South never could succeed. I have understood from accused that he was in favour of old government. He formerly said he would remain neutral.

I have never heard accused say anything [in] favour of the South. His associates were men who were opposed to our Government. I am perhaps the only man favourable to Government with whom he associated. We went to school together in the old county. Accused was engaged in enrolling men, at Comfort for frontier defense. He wanted to be 1st lieutenant. The company was not received owing to illegality.

At the next time he was not elected and went away. He came with a lot of men and went away with them; there were more men than could be received. He gave $10.00 I believe to fit out Sibley's Brigade.

The man Kuechler[24] who was to be captain of the company of which, accused was to lieutenant has left his home, gone to the mountains. Disloyal men sometimes have meeting. On the occasion I saw them when accused with them. Most of them, say 70 or 80, have gone off to avoid conscription. They are in the mountains, on the Leona or Perdenalis *(sic)*; from his conversation I judged accused to be more in favour of the North than the South.

By the accused.

I know that accused put himself to raise men for Sibley's Brigade. I know that accused furnished all the equipment for men for the Brigade. I remember that accused told me, if his men, who he then commanded, would elect him captain; he would go into the Confederate Service.

At the time I believe no one mistrusted accused. I believe that he told me that he had applied for a commission to raise a company for frontier defense.

Accused was said "no matter who got the commission, I would take a change and run for 1st lieutenant.

Accused was not asked about his political sentiments, as others when the company was raised. The men, who I saw at the meeting with the accused, were those that have run off. Those men generally come to town, on Sundays. Accused generally goes to Doebbler's,[25] where the meetings were to get beer. Accused has been in the habit of going to that house for 8 or 10 years.

I believe that those men were discussing politics. At first accused said he would keep neutral, but for the last 3 months he has talked otherwise. I know that accused had hard words with men who trying to keep him out of office.

Accused told me that [Van der] Stucken[26] would try to keep men out of service to beat him. The man, who was arrested, was arrested on a capias [habeas corpus?], for fine by the District County. I don't think he wanted to arrest the man to keep him out of the service. This was about five months, when the man was arrested, after the fine was imposed. I did not see the party when he was beaten.

[Hilmar] Gersdorff[27] sworn says:

About the last half of May 1862, accused told me I ought not to sell my wool now, for the reason that Confederate Money would be worth nothing in fourteen days. On one occasion he told me he was as good a Southern man as anybody. He came to my house sometimes and had bad news, was the reason, why I asked the question, whether he was in favor of the South.

By the Accused.

I have not been friendly with the accused at all times, but have been friends for the last year. There was no one present when this conversation occurred.

I believe that I repeated this conversation about the money in some store, in Fredericksburg. Accused told me as a private friend that Confederate Money would be worth nothing in fourteen days. I understood his object was to prevent me from squandering my property. He also told me to wait a little longer and then sell the wool. He told me that now was not the right time to sell wool. He called himself my friend and I supposed he was talking for my good. My understanding was that he thought the money was worthless, and not the low price. Accused has always whenever I have talked with, believed that the South was too weak to win the contest.

Confederate Military Commission - 1862

Charles Nimitz,[28] sworn says:

I have reason to believe that accused tried to keep men out of the service. There was an attempt to get up a company for the service and accused was defeated in becoming its commander, and through the influence of some persons, the company was disbanded by the Governor.

All those men, nearly without exception, refused to join any other company and I believe through the defendant's influence. From that day to this time, accused, (as I believe) has used his influence on those young men and nearly all of them are now in the woods.

I know accused well and I would not call him loyal. Accused is not regarded by any loyal men of Gillespie County as being loyal himself. Accused is an intelligent man and I think his Influence is great among the illiterate. The accused is an active man and has something to say on all passing events. His associates for the last few months have been those whose loyalty is doubted.

By the accused.

At the time the Frontier Company was raised, you (meaning accused) raised men secretly. It is customary when companys *(sic)* are to be raised, to give notice. When this company was raised none could find it out, except those who were to join it, and persons who made inquiries, were told falsehoods as to the time and place of meeting. In place of holding their meetings at Fredericksburg, they went to Comfort 22 miles below and held their meeting.

20

I never had any list of men in my hands showing the progress made by the accused in raising the company. I call myself loyal and the Hunter Brothers[29] loyal. I call all those loyal who worked to break up that company by petition to the Governor.

I never saw any notice given by accused that he was going to raise a company. Accused and I have very strong difficulties. I have noticed that when accused heard conversations at my table favorable to the South that he would try to change it.

At the time Sibley's Brigade was raised, Captain [Gustav] Schleicher[30] came up he did not get a company, but got 12 or 13 men. Accused was one of the Committee to raise money and outfit these men. So far as we knew, he was regarded loyal at that time. I thought so.

At the time questions were propounded to Kuechler we did not propound them to accused, because we did not believe the Organization would succeed. I have known accused 11 years. Accused is considered a reserved man.

By Judge Advocate

The difficulty between us was about the petition we sent to the Governor. He denounced all who were engaged in it and said they were all a damn click, but he could bring 200 men to our doors and make us talk differently. The reason we wanted the company disbanded was that we did not want the officers commissioned. From their expression we did not believe them loyal. It was signed by about 28 men.

I know of a young man being beaten, for lending Mr. [James] Hunter[31] a horse. Accused was present when it was done. Hunter was elected 1st lieutenant and the man loaned Hunter his horse and was beaten for it.

Accused was present and sheriff at the time. There was a meeting of young men about the 18th May, at which loud expressions were uttered against the Confederacy. The accused being present, the gathering was at a Beer and Wine Shop, they committed a great many excess, cursed and abused the Secession Dogs, and said they would whip them out. Accused did not interfere when the young man was whipped, although present and sheriff at the time. Accused was a participant at the meeting on Sunday he had been drinking with them.

I was not present when the young man was beaten, but I have heard all about it from more than twenty reliable men. I was not present and did not see the men at the meeting, but George Weinheimer[32] was present. It was the same day the man fell from his horse and broke his head.

Frederic Fresenius,[33] being sworn, says:

I know that the accused was engaged in getting up a company, at the time the Frontier Regiment was raised. There were a great many who intended to join the company, but could not find out where or when they would meet. They met, about 20 miles from Fredericksburg and organized. These men now, the greater part, are positively against us. A few have joined other companies, but the balance of the men are out in the woods and cannot be found.

He is now considered as disloyal by the loyal people of the town the others may consider themselves as loyal to Lincoln. One of the young men who joined the company, said that their object was to join and when the Yankees come they would lay down their arms. I take it that those men were disloyal from the fact as soon as Martial Law was declared; they all put out, and have not shown themselves since. Those men have shown their disloyalty ever since Secession, but after that company was broken up, they have shown their disloyalty and insulted us. I believe accused disloyal at the time from the fact that he never came near us any more. I should think accused knew of all the objects of the company, because they were all of the same stripe.

Engelbert Krauskopf[34] sworn says:

I have heard accused make remarks which led me to believe that he was opposed to us. He always went with the opposition or Union party. I know one time there was a Methodist Preacher, who came in and spoke about the war, and said he believed the war would be over in six weeks. He always meets with the party who halloes for he Union.

* * *

July 23, 1862

The Commission imposed a fine of Ten $10.00 Dollars upon Captain Frank van der Stucken for absenting himself from the Commission after being duly summoned as a witness in the above case, and he stands committed until the fine and cost are paid.

Henry S. W. Basse[35] being sworn says:

I know nothing against accused. I don't know of his having advised anyone not to take Confederate Money.

By the Accused.

The general opinion was against you as regards the South. I can't say that you have done anything against the South, to justify such opinions. I mean the general opinion was, that accused was disloyal to the South.

Captain Frank van der Stucken being sworn says:

I think in general, accused is a disloyal subject. At the time my company was mustered into the Confederacy, he attempted to keep one of my men out of the service, by arresting him, as Sherriff. He had allowed the man to go for months, and just at the time he was joining my company he came and arrested him. His associates are men of his own stamp. He being head boss. He is regarded so by the loyal people living near him.

The bulk of the men who composed Kuechler's Company are now in the woods. There are a few of them in my company, I believe the company was gotten up for proper purpose. I have not heard accused say anything by which I could judge that he was disloyal. I know there was a writ formerly, I did not know it then.

Two months previous to this you came to me for some money for Schwartz[36]. You asked me if Schwartz had any money with me. You did not get the money. I raised my company 1st of May.

* * *

July 24, 1862

For Defense.

Dr. Wilhelm Victor Keidel[37] of Gillespie County being duly sworn says:

At the time Schleicher was raising a company, you were active in assisting to get up the men. The reputation of Mr. Nimitz is good as regards truth and veracity. In all business matters he will tell the truth; but if he wants a little fun he will joke sometimes.

In speaking of reports about town, if Nimitz's name was mentioned in connection, it was generally believed. In regard to late political movements when Nimitz mentioned them they were believed, he took nothing from the air. I know nothing of your intentions in raising the company.

I addressed question to Mr. Kuechler in regard to his opinions. I did think of addressing them to you. We have had some conversation but I don't remember about them. You expressed your opinion freely against me.

I think you would act as you express yourself. You had quarrels with the Chief Justice. I believe Nimitz will tell the truth on oath.

Ottocar Miller[38] sworn says:

You accused frequently come into my store. Accused has exercised a bad influence over Kuechler's Company, since it was broke up. Those men left in a lump and are now out it the woods, they were influenced by accused. It is my opinion and the opinion of most loyal citizens where accused lives, that he is not loyal to the South.

When Kuechler first got a commission to raise a company, there was an advertisement put up but there was no time of meeting specified. Kuechler is not at home, he is believed to be in the woods with those young men.

He left home when Duff's Company was there.

Mr. [Frederick] Wrede[39] being sworn says:

I know the accused has assisted getting up means to support soldiers. He appeared to be very active in collecting means. It is said that he has so expressed himself, that no other conclusion could be drawn than, that he was dissatisfied with the things that be.

I have heard that on account of personal difficulties, he had been accused of disloyalty. You so expressed yourself to me.

You assured me that you had done as much as anyone else to support the Confederacy. This was after the frontier company was broken up. You express your opinions freely. I don't think any of the men who have testified against accused, would tell a falsehood against him, because of personal dislike. I could not believe that any man had perjured himself unless I was known to the fact.

Charles Schwartz being sworn, says:

You had a Warrant from District Court of Gillespie County against me. At the time of the District Court I was not at home. I got back a few days before new years. At the time you was raising your company, you told me if I would join the company, you would make it good. You told me afterwards that I would have to pay it and on my saying that I would pay it out the first money, he said it was good. I offered my father-in-law as security, I did not give him, you did not come and ask for it. I promised you a Power of Attorney to get the pay. I did not give it, nor did I give it to you.

You refused to go with me to get a Power of Attorney, for my bounty, which I offered you. The next day I was arrested.

I had to give [van der] Stuckey a Power of Attorney to get back the money which he paid to accused to get me released. You would have put me in jail if it had not have been for Stucken, who paid the money. I paid the money in your house same day.

I never heard that the company would lay down their arms when the Yankees come. There is about 14 or 15 of his old company in our company. The men from Live Oak or Pedernales were opposed to your election. Those who are now in our company were for you for office, I don't know where the men are who voted against you.

Mr. Slessinger[40] [Adam Schuesslar?] being duly sworn, says:

At the time Duff's Company was in Fredericksburg you was there for several days off and on.

R. J. Radcliff being sworn says:

It was very noisy when you came in where the men were drunk on the Sunday, and as soon as you came it, all was silent. You put a man, by the name of Patch [Joseph Poetsch?[41]], out of the house who was riding in.

F. W. Doebbler being sworn says:

You came into my house about one hour before supper. There had been a great deal of drunkenness in my house that day. When you came into my house you came in and tried to quell the disturbance. You staid in my house from an hour to an hour and a half.

This was the same day that Mr. [Oscar] Basse[42] was insulted. I believe you was out during the time. Basse was not in the house.

There was no one hallooed for Lincoln or the Union, that day in my house. If they had talked politics I would have prevented it. I don't know that there are any about

Fredericksburg, disloyal to the South. I believe all the people of Fredericksburg are loyal to the South.

I don't believe that there are any persons in Gillespie County who are disloyal to the South. I like to take Confederate Money.

I know of none who do not like to take it. There are a portion of three companies in service. I don't believe there are any absent from Gillespie County who are not in the army. I don't know where Kuechler is. His farm is four or five miles from town. I am 36 or 37 years old and am a citizen of the Confederate States.

Gustav Schleicher being sworn says:

When I was in Fredericksburg in the fall, you raised several men for my company. You was one of a committee to raise money to equip the men. Your minute company was out on the drill on Sunday, he address them and urged them to join Mr. Schleicher Company. I head a good many remarks made in Fredericksburg that you were against the South. You told me that these remarks were not right, that they were actuated by personal malice.

You told me if the enemy came, you would prove your loyalty. You have the reputation of expression your opinions too freely sometimes. It is likely that if you were opposed to the South, you would have spoken it at sometime. I thought at the time, accused was honest in his expressions.

* * *

July 26, 1862

Mr. [August] Siemering[43] being duly sworn says:

I know that Captain Walker[44] was sent to Fredericksburg to reorganize a militia company. Some one was sent to Llano County to reorganize a company. The Governor told me this. The Governor said there had been foul play in getting up these companies.

Nimitz, Fresenius and Wahrmund[45], signed the petition. I don't believe these men would swear a falsehood.

You tried to get men into Captain Walker's Company. I exchanged some Treasury Warrants for Confederate Money, for accused and at his instance.

The parties did not think it necessary to address questions to accused as they did to others. I had no doubt about his loyalty. I heard nothing said about disloyalty of accused. They knew that accused was going to marry a sister-in-law of mine.

* * *

The Prisoner Philip Braubach being brought before the Commission, offered the following defense.

30

Confederate States vs. Philip Braubach

San Antonio

July 27th, 1862

To the Military court in session San Antonio.

Being charged with disloyalty for having arrested Charles Schwartz, I will not refer you to his testimony, which is without any doubt in my favor, but I simply say, "I have done my duty as Sheriff."

In regard to the Depreciation of the Currency, I do not deny the conversation with Mr. Gersdorff, but I deny of having the intention to depreciate it, as Mr. Gersdorff states himself. With these two points, the Charge of Disloyalty was specified by the Court and if no new questions had been introduced, I would have finished my argument with these few words. But as the case is now, I will call the attention of the Court to some of the testimonies.

Mr. Wahrmund, Fresenius and Nimitz accused me of being disloyal and sustain this accusation in the following manner.

1. He raised a party of men for service in the frontier regiment, who were believed to be opposed to the Southern Government, and had some secret understanding among themselves; one of them say, to lay down their arms, if Northern troops should come. He heard it from a man who got it from another one, who is not to be found. (I supposed the Noble Gentleman got it from the San Antonio News, June 15th) Captain V. D. Stucken and Charles Schwartz told you, that these men were raised for the protection of the frontier, to

fight the enemy and that these very same men, who I have raised are now proving to be in the service of the Confederate States, that they are not opposing but supporting our Government.

2. It was by his influence that the same party of men did not enter into the frontier regiment. If these men had have been opposed to our Government it would have been very well, having kept them out of the service, but as I have proved they were not disloyal. I refer the court to Lt. Siemering, who says, I have tried to get my men mustered into the service and that they have not joined, because the enrolling officer did not act fairly. These three witnesses in signing a petition to the Governor gave their reasons in their own handwriting, why this company must be disbanded and reorganized. The Court knows the contents of the petition and heard their statements.

The petition was not sworn to and these gentlemen had a right to say what they pleased, as the Court informs me. But as I believe the Military Court is not under the strict rules of District Courts and would be willing to find out by all means, whether the Defendant is Guilty or not. I suppose this will be admissible, if not as testimony though as argument. It shows at least that these witnesses are able to make different statements on the same subject, in different places and at different times. A noble thinking man will always say the truth, if on oath or not. What may induce these gentlemen to testify in such a manner against me. Is it malice, hate, or have a few cowardly deserters of the Conscription Law put them in such a furious state that their mind is disturbed, as it seemed to be the case. I turn with disgust from this whole machination, and leave the question at once.

Where has a solitary action been shown, a solitary remark been heard, by which disloyalty could be proved? But some of the witnesses have told you that I have supported the government with my time, labor and money. I gave $10.00 or $20.00 and a whole outfit, horse saddle and bridle and a six shooter to equip volunteers. By my interventions, public conversations, which were unfavourable to the South, have been turned. I have declared that I was a good Southern man and am known to express myself at all times most too freely and regardless of consequences. Why Gentlemen, if I am disloyal, did I not tell them I was not in favor of the government, I am not a Southern man, did not want to live in the country any longer and—gone out of it. I could have easily done it, nothing was in my way. As to the remark, "the South would not succeed" I gave my opinion as freely at all other times and it was impressed on my mind by the defeats of our armies, place and place was taken by the enemy and place after place has been evacuated by our troops and who at that time, when the matter stood _____ for our arms, was not in fear we might be overpowered? I was at that time of this opinion and expressed it to good Southern men, as I am not in the habit of keeping back my opinions.

But there is one more question. "He is disloyal because he does not appear in our society." Mr. Fresenius says in the same testimony at the same time "I never kept society with him, I did not care for it." Mr. Miller had very little to do with me, did not want my society, I was too overbearing for him. Mr. Wrede does not appear in society. I had not spoken for 18 months with Mr. Krauskopf, have had very strong difficulties with Mr. Nimitz. Who now remains of this club of loyal witnessed? Mr. Wahrmund! And I kept his company. But I was in the society of Mr. Radcliff. Of course I was, and I did prefer his society for years past and I do so today.

Now to come to any end with the whole matter, I will state to the Court that I have been deprived of my liberty since 7 weeks and been chained down during the whole time with two heavy balls. I was treated in the roughest manner possible, no bedding, no clothes were allowed me, until I had been imprisoned already for a long time, although I had asked several times of these necessary comforts of life. I have suffered innocently and I would entreat the Court not to let me suffer any longer in such a manner and to pass a judgement.

I fully submit to justice and remain
Signed
Philip Braubach

* * *

July 28, 1862

Charge 1st
"Disloyalty."
Specification 1st

In arresting men who were in debt; making this the austensible *(sic)* reason; but really to prevent men from serving the Country, in the Capacity of Soldiers, he being Sherriff at the time.

Charge 2nd
"Depreciating Confederate Money"
Specification 1st
In stating to H. V. Gersdorff, that the Currency of the Country, meaning thereby Confederate Money, would be worth nothing at all and advising him not to sell his wool for it, as in fourteen days it would be worth nothing.

Duly submitted
Singed John Ireland
Judge Advocate and Recorder

In the foregoing case of Confederate States vs. Philip Braubach, the evidence being concluded, the defendant submitted his defense, whereupon *(sic)* the Office of the Commission was cleared and the vote being put on Charge 1st the Commission find the accused "Guilty."

On Specification first,
"Not Guilty" owing to the discrepancy between the proof and the specification.

On Charge 2nd "Guilty"

Specification first.
"Guilty"

And the Commission sentence said Braubach to imprisonment for period of ninety days and to pay a fine of $200.00 to stand committed until the fine is paid.

* * *

August 4, 1862.

Confederate States vs. Braubach

In this case the sentence and findings of the Commission having been disapproved by the General Commanding (Brigadier General H. P. Bee), and the case being recommitted to the Commission, and said case coming up for reconsideration, the Commission find the said Braubach, on

Charge 1st
"Guilty"
Specification 1st
"Not Guilty"
Specification 2nd
"Guilty"
Charge 2nd
"Guilty"
Specification 1st
"Guilty"

And the Commission sentence said Braubach, to imprisonment for and during the period of the present war, then to be sent out of Confederate States and never to return, under penalty of death.

August 8, 1862 - Special Order No. 409
The Confederate States vs. Philip Braubach

In this case, the Military Commission in session at San Antonio, before whom it was tried, having found the said Braubach, "Guilty" on the Charges of "Disloyalty" and "Depreciation of the Confederate Currency" and having sentenced him to "imprisonment for and during the period of the present war, then to be sent out of the Confederate States, not to return under the penalty of Death."

Therefore, the findings are hereby approved, but the sentence is hereby ordered to be modified to imprisonment for the period of the War."

By Order of Brigadier General H. P. Bee
Signed E. F. Gray
Major and A.A.A. General

July 22, 1862 - Case 18
Confederate States[46] vs. Frederick Lochte[47]

Frederick Dambach[48] a witness in this case being duly sworn deposed as follows:

I was indebted to the accused, had a chance to dispose of three cows to pay the debt. I went near the house of accused, and found accused, who said "no paper Money."

The accused said at least on old debts I will not take the money. I again went to Lochte with a witness and tendered the money again, when accused said, you can't compel me to take the money now, and he would not take it, and witness walked off.

This was about the first days of June 1862. It was Confederate paper that I tendered to accused. I had the money out on table in the presence of the accused and it was spread out, so Lochte could see distinctly what sort of money it was. Here some Bills are spread on the table before the Commission and witness says "it was so," that he acted with Lochte.

By accused.

Accused told me (witness) before I exhibited the Money, that he did want to collect his debts. Accused said he did not want trouble, or something to that effect.

I had been indebted to accused about two years, or maybe more. Accused has at diverse times asked me for the money, of this I am certain. Since the Note was given he never asked for Money.

The Note was given about one and a half years ago. Accused saw the Money on the table being right at it, and must have seen it, I am no Merchant; but the Money I tendered was no common paper.

Accused said at this time, he did not collect his old debts; this was at the same time that I tendered the Money.

I am certain that accused said to witness, "at all events no paper money." This was said at the commencement of the first conversation. Witness replied that there was no other Money in the country but that kind. Accused has the reputation of being rich and is a close collector.

[Ludwig] Dambach[49] (sworn) says;

I went with my father when he put Confederate Money on the table, making accused a tender, and he refused to receive it. I believe that accused knew that it was Confederate Money, for my Father put it out on the table.

Lochte told my Father that he would collect no debts, that he followed the law. My Father had previously make Lochte a tender of the Money. Witness knew that it was Confederate Money. The Bills were laid open on the table.

By the accused.

Witness was in the house with the parties, when it occurred, was in such a situation that he could see. Lochte left the room.

James P. Waldrip[50] (being duly sworn), deposed as follows:

I went into Lochte to buy some tobacco; he said he did not have any. I then asked him if he would sell me some shingles I saw at the door, he said he would sell them to me. I told him that I would return and pay him for them. He said very well. I returned in a few days and brought my wagon to get the shingles, he was at the Gin. I told him that I had nothing less the $20.00; he said that he did not want the money; but would take a cow and calf.

I told him I could sell the cow for more than he could give, and that I did not want to sell cows. I don't think I showed the money. I think I told him that I had a $20.00 Confederate bill. I think he would have taken it if it had not been for his wife. I don't speak or understand German. There was no one present except Lochte, his wife, and myself. There were two others off pressing wool. These men were some 30 feet off from where we were, and I don't think heard what was said. Lochte was still willing to sell the singles. It was after I had told him nothing less than $20.00 bill, that he said he would rather use the Shingles. There was but little other money in circulation than Confederate money. This was about the 6th day of June 1862.

If I had had the Gold or Silver, I would have got the shingles, or he refused to receive Confederate Money, he knew I had it in my pocket.

I bought the shingles previously and it was only when he knew what sort of money I had, that he refused to let me have them.

By the Accused.

Lochte asked me about a month prior to this, if I would sell him some cows. Mr. Lochte said nothing about cows, when I bought the shingles, nor did he say, he wanted a cow for them, when I went for them. When I approached, I said to him "I have come for those shingles." After I had told him that I had no change and nothing less than $20.00. Mr. Lochte speaks English well enough for me to trade with him.

I cannot say that Mr. Lochte did not understand me, but I do know that if I had had the Gold or Silver, that I would have got the shingles. And I know more, at the time he met me in the street and asked me if I would sell some cows; I told him I would not sell him some cows. Accused is a merchant and I never had any difficulty in trading with him.

* * *

July 23, 1862

The evidence having closed, the Office of the Commission was cleared the Commission fined on 1st Charge—"Guilty"

Specification of 1st Charge.—"Guilty"
Specification of 2nd Charge.—"Guilty"

Wherefore the Commission sentenced said Lochte to Thirty five (35) days imprisonment and to pay a fine of One $100.00 Hundred Dollars, to remain in Prison until the fine is paid.

July 24, 1862 - Case 12
Confederate States[51] vs. J. R. Radcliff

Lt. James Hunter being sworn says:

I have heard accused make remarks often, from which I could draw no other conclusion than that he was opposed to the South.

In speaking if the currency would depreciate, we were in business together and he urged me to get rid of all Confederate Money, as that as soon as the first battle was fought the money would go down.

I often spoke to him, asked him to change his course, he said he could not, it was impossible. There was a great deal said, but this is the substance. These conversations have been carried on repeatedly by accused, with others, about the Store, against remonstrance.

This was during the last year, up to about the last of December. This was in Fredericksburg, Texas. On the subject of slavery he always said he was opposed to slavery, though he said he never would interfere with it, nor do I believe he would.

He said he fully coincided with J. Ulrich[52] (who resided in San Antonio) on the subject of slavery. I think from his remarks that it was not only his opinion, but that it was his desire that we should be whipped in the first great battle.

I draw this conclusion from his remarking, after hearing of one of our victories, that this confounded Confederacy would exist and that if it did he would leave the country.

He never appeared to credit any favorable report to the South. He is a man very much beliked where he lives, and in all other respects he is thought a great deal of. He has a large influence over his neighbors.

By the accused.

I never heard you say in so many words that you wanted the South whipped.

I have heard you make use of remarks, "confound the Confederacy," or remarks to that effect. This was on hearing of one of our victories. I never knew you to commit any direct act against the Confederacy. We did deliver corn and beef to the government as well here as in Louisiana. I don't remember any dispute between us about the money. We were speaking of Slave and free labor. You said that slavery was doomed, that you thought free labor would pay better and was preferable. I don't remember that you said if we could accounts from both sides, we would get about the truth.

I thought that he did not place in confidence in our accounts of battles, was the reason why he made the remarks as above. I know that reports in papers are often untrue, which are always corrected.

Accused urged his opinions and never conceded anything. My brother told accused that he was sorry that he taken the course he had and would like to see him change, the accused remarked, "can the Leopard change his spots." This I heard in December last.

Dr. Keidel being sworn says:

I don't think accused very loyal; We have often conversed on the state of the country. I have forgotten a great deal. When we read news of our victories he always doubted, until doubt was beyond reach. He never believed that the Confederacy would succeed.

By Accused.

I have never known you to commit any act against the Confederate Government. I think you generally obey the laws.

Mr. Henry Basse sworn says:

On one occasion I heard Radcliff say he was for the Union. He was for the Union and wanted to stick to it. This was after secession. I heard this expression myself. You filled all your contracts with the Government.

I know that you have received Confederate Money in the last few months.

Mr. Charles Nimitz being sworn says:

He (accused) has often argued against the course the Government had taken, and against the basis of our currency.

I mean that he was opposed to the Government itself. He did not believe the money worth what it called for. We had had so many disputes that I can't remember any particular remarks. In these arguments and disputes, I have but seldom if every heard him say anything in favor of our Government.

By the Accused.

I have heard you say that the currency was based on the Confidence of the people. You have made so many arguments against the Government and made bets against its ability to maintain itself, that I can't specify. Witness boarded accused.

The tendency of the course of accused was to bring the government into disrepute.

He told me on one occasion that if knew the sentiments of the people, as well as he did, that I would not hoist the Confederate Flag on my house. He was displeased. We were then on friendly terms. This I regarded as a friendly act.

John M. Hunter[53] sworn says:

I have had a great many arguments relating to the troubles. He has always argued against me and in favor of the Union. He has always said that the North would certainly subjugate the South, there was no other chance.

He was very much dissatisfied about the secession of the South; I have often asked him to change his course, he replied, "Can the Leopard change his spots." I know his opinions if any person does and I have not idea that he would fight against the Starts and Stripes and unless he has changed very much since I last saw him, he would be delighted to see them flying over this country. I conversed with accused the last time about February last. About this time he quit his old associates and went with Braubach and Doebbler.

By the Accused.

I think I have heard you say that you did not want to take any hand in this conflict, that it as an unnatural one. I think he told me himself at one time he did not like to argue any further upon the subject and he would go with those who would not oppose him. I have heard your remark that Slavery was a very bad institution and that it would be abolished, but that you would not interfere with it. You have always taken paper money.

Ratcliff came to me and said the news had come; the paper money was at a discount. Money can be depreciated by remarks as will as by refusing to take it.

He is very free to express himself, he talks to most anybody. You asked my previous to this, to settle this money affair with Basse.

P. H. Braubach being sworn says:

I heard Mr. Hunter say to Ratcliff that he had no right whatever with the business and that the business was carried on by him and his brother. You were always ready to bet on almost every subject. I remember that you remarked that the

South would be justified in setting aside the "Habeas Corpus" Act, as the North had done the same thing.

I know that you have received Confederate Money. I have heard you remark after that, that newspapers reports could not be trusted. I don't remember that I every hear you say "confound the Government."

Nimitz has the reputation of stating reports that are not true. I don't believe Nimitz would swear a lie, when he is not interested.

* * *

July 26, 1862

In this case the Judge Advocate has to submit the following.

The proof in this case is so clear and explicit that the accused is not only a Black Republic, but that he is always active in disseminating his opinions, that it is not thought necessary to recite particular occasions or acts.

His partners in business, who now appear to be attached him, corroborate other witness as to Defendants' disloyalty to the South, and to his being by nature a Black Republican.

The proof is that he is active in speaking his mind, that he is a merchant a men beliked and calculated to do the government infinite harm. He has sought the public hotels and other places of resort to make his opinions known. The most significant fact in the case is that the defendant fails to bring any witness to show one word or [deed] he ever done or spoke in favor of this government. As the Leopard is for spotted, so is defendant an Abolitionist. These men have rent asunder the fairest government, man ever beheld, and shall we now allow them to remain, in our Country, or permit them to return after war, to reinact *(sic)* for use, or our children, the occurrences of the last two years on this continent.

Charge 1st
"Disloyalty"
Specification first.

In this, that in conversation in Fredericksburg about three months after the passage of the ordinance of secession and at sundry other times, said Ratcliff stated, that he could not change his mind, and he was opposed to the government meaning thereby the Government of the Confederate States.

An further that during the months of March and April or about that period of the year 1862 and at other times shortly previous, he openly and frequently expressed himself opposed to the Confederate Government.

Charge 2nd
"Depreciation of the Currency"
Specification second.

In this that about three months ago, or thereabouts said Radcliff has stated publicly on one or more occasions, that the paper currency, meaning thereby, the money of the Confederate Government, had no basis and there was nothing to redeem it with and further, that in his conversations generally he endeavored to impress persons unfavorable towards the Government and its credit.

Signed John Ireland
Judge Advocate and Recorder

The accused, J. Radcliff, then presented the following defense:

To the Military Court
San Antonio

Gentlemen

In conformity with your orders, I submit to you the following remarks on the evidence in my case, now pending before you.

Though it appears from the evidence, that I have talked about politics, doubted newspaper reports and still, none of all the witness brought, could say that I ever committed an illegal act or an act of hostility to the existing government, nay Mr. John M. Hunter, who had known me for the last three or four years, expressly states that he does not consider me able to do such an act.

The evidence further shows that the expressions, which I am said to have made, were made in the year 1861, none was proved against me since that, and Mr. J. M. Hunter says that I tried to avoid argument (February and March 1862). On the remarks in regard to my opinion about Slavery, contained in the evidence of Messrs. Hunter, I do not need to dwell, as the evidence of these gentlemen themselves, shows how inoffensive these opinions were.

Confederate States vs. J. R. Radcliff

As to the 2nd Charge it appears that I have argued in private circles about the paper currency of the Confederates, but it would not be ridiculous to suppose, that I had done so with a view of depreciating the currency, while I, jointly with my partner had Corn and Beef Contract to the army of about $3,000? Besides was not the rate of Exchange of Confederate Paper against Gold quoted in the New Orleans papers till lately? And does not every obligation of a State, change more or less in the market?

Hoping soon to get a judgement in this case, I am
Gentlemen
Your Obedient Servant

Signed - Rudolph Radcliff

San Antonio - July 26th 1862
Case No. 12 - Confederate States vs. J. R. Radcliff

The proof in this case being through, and the commission being cleared, the question was put on Charge 1st upon which Commission say "Guilty"

Specification 1st   "Guilty"
Charge 2nd   "Guilty"
Specification 1st   "Guilty "

Where the Commission sentence the accused to Banishment from the limits of the Confederate States, and that he never return thereto, under the penalty of death.

51

Confederate Military Commission - 1862

The following letter was addressed by the Judge Advocate to the prisoner, J. R. Radcliff

Office of the Military Commission
San Antonio, August 2nd 1862

J. R. Radcliff

Your petition to the General Commanding (General H. P. Bee) has been handed me with a request to answer it. I am instructed to say that your request cannot be granted, but that any facility in settling your affairs, consistent with the public welfare, will be granted.

Signed John Ireland
Judge Advocate July 25, 1862

July 25, 1862 -Case 8
Confederate States[54] vs. H. J. Richarz[55]

There being no proof to convict the Prisoner of any offense, he was discharged from custody this day.

July 30, 1862 - Case No. 5
Confederate States[56] vs. Blasins Kieffer[57]

The accused in the above case being brought before the Commission on the 24th instant there being no testimony against him and the accused being an ignorant man and not liable to military duty, he was discharge from custody.

July 30, 1862 – Case 6
Confederate States[58] vs. Joseph Wipff[59]

The accused in the above case being brought before the Commission was found to be an ignorant man and was therefore discharge from custody.

September 20, 1862 – Case 43
Confederate States⁶⁰ vs. Eduard Degener⁶¹

The Case was called and fixed for trial, for Monday the 22 September 1862.

September 22, 1862

The above case was continued on motion of defendant's attorney until Saturday, September 27, 1862.

September 26, 1862

Now comes the Defendant Eduard Degener and [objects?] to the jurisdiction of this court and respectfully protests against any action of the same in regard to him, for this:

That said court is an illegal and an unauthorized body.

That all of its acts and proceeding are in violation of the Constitution of the Confederate States and of this state.

Waelder & Upson of
Counsel for Defendant
September 27, 1862

In this cause the prisoner was brought into open court and thereupon the Judge Advocate read to him the charges and specifications against him as follows:

Charge—that Eduard Degener is hostile to the Government of the Confederate States, and is a dangerous and seditious person and an enemy to the government of the Confederate State.

Specification 1.

That in the month of August 1862 in this State, the said Eduard Degener, had knowledge of the existence of band of men, in the counties of Kerr, Gillespie, Comal, Kendall, and Blanco, and other counties, who were hostile to the Government of the Confederate States and were arming themselves for the purpose of fighting here and escaping into Mexico when they desired, and that so knowing he failed to give information of such conspiracy to the proper authorities.

Specification 2.

In this the said Eduard Degener by false seditious exaggerated and slanderous written statements sought in August 1862, in this state to bring Confederate Government into disrepute, and array one class of the population in hostility to the other.

Specification 3.

That the said Eduard Degener had written correspondence with the armed enemies of the Confederate States, and assisted and aided in arming them and fitting them out, the said enemies being the men who fought the Confederate forces under Lt. McRae[62], near the Head of the Nueces River and not far from Fort Clark. All this in about the month of August 1862.

C. S. West
Judge Advocate:

The accused having heard the same pleaded not guilty.

The accused through his counsel then offered a plea to the jurisdiction of the Court, and after due deliberation by the Court the said plea was overruled.

It is further ordered that all the evidence taken in said cause, together with the defense of the Counsel and the reply of the Judge Advocate be recorded as follows:

The accused through his counsel then submitted certain special exceptions of the Charge and the different specifications which at due deliberations were by the Count overruled.

The accused then announced himself ready for the trial on charge and specifications.

Edward Slessinger[63] Esq. was then duly sworn as Interpreter; after proceeding with the examination witness, the Court adjourned until Monday 8:00 a.m. the 29th of September 1862.

[NOTE: The Commission met on September 29, 30, and October 1, and heard evidence in the case of Confederate States vs. Eduard Degener. This evidence and the arguments by both the counsel for the defense and the judge advocate were not given in the court records for those dates, but were summarized in the report after the verdict.]

Edward Slessinger (duly sworn, says) testifies that the letter referred to by P. L. Buquor and Lt. Lilly in their evidence was submitted to him by the Provost Marshal, that it was in the

German language, that he translated it; and a translation being shown to the witness he recognized it as the one he had made; he said the translation, as corrected in lead pencil was correct, and further stated that he was familiar with the German language, and was also quire familiar with the English language, and he for many years been in the habit of writing and speaking both languages.

(Signed) Edward Slessinger
(Translation referred marked "B")

P. L. Buquor[64] (duly sworn) was here shown letter referred to in the testimony of Slessinger and said that he had seen the letter before, that he was Deputy Provost Marshal of San Antonio and that the letter had been passed in to his hands by Lilly and that on the day when the accused was in arrest and brought before him as Provost Marshal for preliminary examination; and when the accused saw the letter he stated that he wrote the letter, before he was asked anything about it. I afterwards asked him if he wrote it and he said he did.
(Signed) P. L. Buquor

[Translation of letter]

August 1, 1862
To: Col. Von Bernewitz,[65] Brunswick
    & Government Counsel Ernst Bramigk-Coethen[66]
You will receive this letter without any heading & without any signature, because I do not know whether it will ever reach you. I am in hopes that you have received my former letter through Dammeit in Hanover & by way of Mexico. The only

object I have in writing, is to inform you that we are all alive & in good health. B's[67] family has been increased by the birth of a charming little daughter. The war, up to the present time has not been in our immediate neighborhood, but [is] not with[out] its inconveniences. The land is divided into Military district, the Chief in each military district having well conceived the duties of a regiment of swords. The Habeas Corpus acts suspended. Summary Martial Justice. Divers Counties nearly stripped of their male population. Every one between the ages of 18 to 35 ordered to take the field, those between 35 & 50 drilled as Militia for future purposes—in exposed parts numbers volunteer for the purpose of carrying on guerilla warfare.[68] This is in consequence of young men having remained true to the Union, and having gone for months into the Mountains and ravines loafing, and followed up and chased by Confederate Troops, like Indians. It is astonishing that their efforts in taking these men prisoners have not been crowned with success. Civil war is on the eve of breaking out.[69] Confederate Troops coming from all sides ascend our mountains. In order to avoid a Vendee war withdrawal across the Rio Grande.—Confiscation acts, imprisonment, Martial Law to the utmost rigor, for all those who do not adjure allegiance to the United States, swear allegiance to the Confederate States, and who do not accept Confederate money as Cash. Those who are compelled to remain here swear, receive a pass; but if he should be of opinion that on account expressions, or on account of his influence among his fellow citizens, he would be placed on the black list, he sleeps in the bushes, has tied to his plough his arms, a horse hitched in the immediate neighborhood, prepared every thing to escape or to hide. To lead such a life is at the commencement very exciting,—then renders a person nervous, then annoying and ultimately becomes second nature.

The crops nearly all over the Country are a failure. Corn $2 ¾ per bushel, each bushel weighing 56 lb.; 100 lb. Flour $15.00; Powder $8.00 per lb. Each shot from a gun, after close calculation cost 7 ½ silbergroschen. No clothing procurable— Quite a common calico Dress, cost 2 months ago $8.00—say 12 Prussian dollars. One pair of shoes like those worn by our workman, on the other side 15 Prussian dollars, in the Capital of the land, Austin. All the former germans cobblers tan beef hides & furnish shoes at $5= 7 ½ Prussian and with all that. This leather is poorly tanned outside, inside it is the rawhide; the price of this so called leather is $1.50; this is my last sheet of paper, no more to be had, no more coffee in the house, none for the last 12 month. Our sweetning, wild honey. The sale of intoxicating liquors prohibited. The last whiskey—say whiskey—which I had cost $3.00 per bottle. We all wear, even the ladies, since Christmas last Moccasins; the pantaloons and coats of men and boys made out of Deerskins tanned by ourselves. Yesterday although with a heat of 30 degrees and losing the meat I had to kill a beef for the purpose of making a lariat in order to hitch horses. For months no rain. Creek all dry, the Guadalupe river appears like a creek, further down it is said she is dry for 15 miles. Grass is brown & altogether disappears. For the last six weeks the wheat has been laying tied up in the field & is waiting for men to thrash it. The merchants having stocks on hand are amassing an enormous quantity of paper money.

The people of the south curse the once beloved United States, and prepared to fight for their rights—"Slavery, or to die in the attempt." About the events in Europe we learn nothing, nothing at all, the news papers bring news of victories, of retreats on account of strategic purposes. We have killed more people to judge by the press, than the population of the north. What will the end to be—. You who are at a distance are perhaps better enable to form an opinion of our position, than we who are in the midst of it. My opinion is as yet the same, when it will come to pass however—qui vivera, verra (who lives will see). In Arkansas they have established a tariff of prices for necessaries of life. The same thing is announced to take place here.

The Military Chiefs i.e. the Provost Marshals have by virtue of a Proclamation emanated from headquarters, the right to act at discretion with suspicious persons. The troops from the South express openly the threat that they will not make any more prisoners; what this means, an American is only able to say. If the south is victorious, it may become necessary for the Germans to emigrate again.[70] In what direction then? The proposition was made in a San Antonio, yesterday, to make good the loss of a freed nigger to each planter, by giving him two Hessians to cultivate his land. As ridiculous as such an observation may be it shows, nevertheless, the hatred of the Southerners towards the "Dutch." They are all considered Black Republicans that means opposed to Slavery; and the fact that Siegel with his Missouri Germans has had so many successes is very maddening to them,[71] as each southern Shopkeeper lawyer is a gentleman and General at their birth.

Who every carries this letter over the Rio Grande and arrives there safe shall sign this letter. Compliments to all friends and relatives and remember us Kindly, even if you do not receive news from us for a long time. Hearty Greetings,—Colonel von Bernewitz in Brunswick and Government Counsel Ernest Bramigk-Coethen. A Blockade is anyhow a ridiculous thing.

At the commencement of March a hail storm took away all my window glasses, with the exception of those on the North and & west side of my house and made my shingle roof like a sive *(sic)*; it is in the same fix this day, because San Antonio affords neither Panes of glass nor nails. Do not be astonished at the unconnectedness of my letter.

Yesterday the departure was determined upon, to day the horses were shod, and are saddled. One Pack Mule carries Provisions for 3 weeks for 3 persons who will be joined by 47 others, picked men.[72] One more dinner, then good bye, who knows whether we will meet again. Not a cent of money in the Pocket, thrown amongst Indians and Mexicans robbers, Where Confederate money is of no more avail then in Mexico. All this is Romance enough to satisfy a dancing tea party in Berlin. I smoke a Pipe, covered with rawhide from top to bottom, including the sack containing fire materials, because the juice or the spit has taken possession of the whole pipe. Miserable land where a man can't even buy a pipe. Mama is baking the last bread for some time to come for her dear sons. The Mail to day announces the price of flour at /18.

W. J. Edwards[73] (duly sworn):

The accused asked me if I was in the fight on the Nueces, the fight of the Confederate troops with the "Bushwhacker" in which Lt. McRae commanded. I said I was. He asked me how many we had in the fight, I told him there was 96. He (accused) asked me if I knew whether his sons were killed or not. I told him I did not know, but one man, who was shot in the mouth, was said to be one of his sons—he asked me if we asked them to surrender. I told him we did not, telling him we supposed they would not surrender, for what we had heard. He said he knew the men well, that they were the best shots in the country, and that they would never have surrendered, we never would have whipped them if we had not the advantage—He said that they were right, we were right—they were fighting for their opinions and we for ours. He said that one of his [sons] was killed; he said the oldest or largest, I don't know which one, conversation was had with him when he was under arrest. No orders were given as to refusing quarters to the enemy in the fight—only orders as to the position were to be in; they had about 68 or 69 men I learned—it was before the day light when the fight began.

By the Court:

The Bushwhackers were well armed, men from 18 to 37, saw no one acting commander or givin' order, though it might have been so—I was what appeared to be a muster roll that was taken from them—but I did not read it closely—Lts. McRae and Lilly had it, we stuck the trail of the

Bushwhackers not for from the South fork of the Guadeloupe—it went South west for a while and then north west—there were two trails came together on the second day about 80 miles from where the fight took place. The general direction of the trail was in my opinion toward Eagle Pass— on the Rio Grande.

Cross Examination. The trail was outside of the Settlements, and through what I believe in Indian country—we killed 32 or 33 of them and took no prisoners—some escaped of them, some were wounded as I supposed—The fight began before day light, and then we were ordered to cease, and renew it again at day light.

(Signed) W. J. Edwards

Ernst Kapp[74] *(duly sworn):*

I am acquainted with the accused about 12 years. I have lived in his neighborhood during that period, at time he was friendly, and sometimes not so, at other polite—for the last years the least friendly. Accused was farming, working in the field himself—and besides that he made shingles. He has a wife, a married daughter, and young son about 13 years— before this had had two grown son; he heard that they were both killed in the fight—their names were Hugo and Hillmar. They were both of age—so far as witness knows—accused had no control over them. In business both they acted for themselves. Knows nothing to the cause of their leaving. He expressed it that he preferred to take part with neither side—

but remained neutral. The accused heard that the negroes were to be ordered to fight against the south, he said in a determined manner, that he would fight against the north, take up arms himself for the South—and fight to the bitter end of the war, that a compromise between the North and South was not desirable, only a permanent separation—when the county of Kendell was organized and the election held there sometime last April that these remarks were made. The above conversation came up casually, passing from local topics to this. On one occasion, then in former years ago, when I had purchased a negro girl he said I had done right, and he only regretted he had not the means [?] time I have know him to try to hire negro women from Dr. Ganahl[75] once on Curry's Creek. He can only say that the longer he known the defendant the stronger and more favorable were his views towards slavery. I never hear him express himself opposed to slavery. I never had any conversation with Degener as to his views in regard to the war of any length: he does not regard him a seditious or dangerous person because he paid taxes, took part in election and took the oath.

Cross examination.

Degener's sons left his house in the 1st day of August, they were at the House of witness frequently, their one horse was shod at his Black-Smith shop a day or two before they left. Degener votes at Precinct No. 3 as Sisterdale, only one. My sons responded to the Gov call for volunteers at said Precinct. Degener is an influential man in his neighborhood. He has paid all taxed demanded of him, has taken part in all county elections and thinks he voted in the Congressional election. Prior to him emigration he was opposed to Slavery.

Witness knows that the Prisoner took part in a meeting held at San Antonio to change constitution in 1853 or 1854.[76]

By the Court.

Witness was not present at the meeting and was opposed to it object, has lived in Texas 12 years. Prisoner told him he was opposed to Slavery previous to his emigration.

Defense.

The voting population at precinct No. 3 numbers about 30 never has exceeded that number—he thinks about 12 or 15 between the ages of 18 & 35. There were about 30 voters when the Governor called for troops, my son volunteered, that population, Americans, Germans & Mexican—about 2/3 Germans. I heard Mr. Degener's two sons were killed in the mountains, in the engagement with Lt. McRae, D. C. I do not know of Degener influencing any one to go to the war, neither do I know of his having influenced any one not to go.

(Signed) Ernst Kapp

Ernst Altgelt[77] (duly sworn):

I am acquainted with the accused; I have known him 10 or 11 years, as long as I have been in the country. I know his two sons Hugo and Hillmar. I have known them since '54 since I have come to the upper Country—I know of a conversation which took place between the accused, his son Hugo, and some other of those who went off; the conversation took place at Comfort under gallery of the Post Office in Comfort, in first part of July '62. Hugo Degener[78] and others were there: Murice [Moritz] Weiss[79] was one of them. I advised them in a friendly way to go and take the oath, saying that thought it was after the time, that Graham the Provost Marshall *(sic)* would not be hard with them; the accused came up and joined in conversation at once, taking up my side of argument, and said, "Boys you do wrong behaving as you did," meaning not taking the oath of allegiance. Hugo said an oath must be voluntary oath and here they compel us to take an oath. The accused said you should consider not for yourselves but the welfare of your parents and the whole settlement in general. You may be sure when the authorities compel you to take an oath they have the power to enforce it. Hugo replied, "Suppose we go down and take the oath, it is not that alone but the next thing would be the conscription.' Accused replied the war could not be so dreadful to him. Hugo replied it was not for war, but he did not wish to fight against principles. One of the crowd said they would make cannon food [fodder out of] the Dutch any how. The accused said in reply I know it is hard for many to go, but we Europeans can't complain about a conscript law, because any country on Earth has a right to call upon its citizens to defend it, naming Prussia whose military institutions were universally admired; the accused went on to show of some countries that all classes of men rich and poor alike had to serve and be soldiers, and much more the same effect. He was in earnest in his manner and even solemn. He said they should not let their private opinions influence them in political matter, but they must be governed by the majority of the Country.

Cross Examined:

I have had other conversations with accused as to the subject of the war—one at Sisterdale in February '62—he said he thought we could hardly organize a force sufficient to oppose the North. Accused said to me that he thought that in the war, under all circumstances, the seven Cotton States would maintain their independence, thought it might possible be that the states west of Mississippi might possibly be given up in the treaty. I have heard of meeting on Spring Creek [Bear Creek][80] but never heard of the accused being at any of them. I heard of his son Hugo being there. There were two parties there; I was Secessionist, the other party styled themselves Unionist. The accused was not considered as belonging to any party. I do not know the objects of the meeting. I suppose to avoid conscription.

Ernest Kranmer[81] [Cramer], Telgschmann[82] [Tellgmann], Henry Scherehelm[83] [Schwethelm], Hugh Degener were at the meeting—These are some of the men who went to bushes and were in fight with Lt. McRae.

By the Court:

The accused and his sons were much attached to each other but they, the sons, were very independent and I doubt whether he, the accused, had so much control over them as to prevent them from going, if they had pledged themselves to go.

Witness was a secessionist from the beginning and advocated secession with all his heart.

Ernest Altgelt

Christoph Rhodius[84] (duly sworn) says:

I am a son-in-law of Degener the accused. Witness lives in Sisterdale. Altgelt the last witness lives in Comfort. Accused son Hugo and Hillmar were between 20 and 24. They are both as far as I know killed. Kuechler got authority to raise a company and they enlisted therein; that authority was recalled and Van der Stucken then got authority. They then refused to go with any one else except Kuechler. They [were] determined not to enter any other company nor to be conscripted—they left the Country to avoid Conscription—this was the beginning of their trouble. Degener the accused make an effort to get his sons to take the oath, and did all to have them do so—they were strong headed and set in their opinions and could not be controlled by their father; Degener's sons went up one or twice to defend Degener; when they heard or were informed that he was to hang they went up once or twice. Afterwards it was rumored about the men were holding large meeting up above for the purpose of resisting the authorities, and the accused advised his sons to have nothing to do with them. The sons said he had better go up himself and tell them to disband, that their going up to disband would no good. He replied that he would have nothing to with it—this was when the reports were first circulated about meeting as to the Government. After this accused wrote a letter to them stating that they had better not meet any more.

The boys returned after 8 days from a long hunt, and said his letter did not good, and if he wanted to do anything he had better go up there himself. Accused then concluded to go up there himself, not to the camp but within four or five miles of there. He tried to dissuade some of them from doing any thing more and for all to go home and obey the laws and they did not meet anymore—the accused said to me he would do all he could to break up the meetings and they promised him not to meet anymore.

I first knew of the boys going to Mexico about ½ an hour before they started—they started in the evening. I lived about ¾ miles from the old man, the accused. Degener was there then and his last words to them was that if they did not intend to stay in the country to leave it as quick as possible—that they ought not to rove around in the mountains but go at once. He (the accused) was very much excited by their departure— the accused told his sons in one conversation with them to be good citizens, that was in word what he said. Accused is fifty-two or three years old.

Cross Examined:

Kuechler's Company was for state service. Witness was then shown the letter referred to by Buquor and said it was the accused. I know the accused hand writing, I have seen his hand frequently, it was directed in the margin to Col. Benitwitz and Brouneck. They, the boys, had one pack animal and for three persons to start: the two sons and Tlgschmann [Tellgmann]. His, the accused, referring to the letter, opinion

I have frequently heard him express that the North, never could conquer the South—I never heard him express any other opinion on that subject, and when the news came that the Negroes were to be armed, he said if that was true, he would try to raise a company himself and fight against the North—regard Degener as a good secessionist. The words, "Heart-Greeting" were written by Mrs. Degener. I voted for Union, so did accused both acquiesced in the will of the majority—and went with the state. The accused was more or less supported by his boys—they helped him on the farm and made shingles for him. The accused would not in my opinion have assisted his sons to go if he were able. I mean by the secession, when used as to Mr. Degener, that he is a good citizen and obeys the laws of the state, but do not regard him as a strong secessionist, meaning by that term a man who lays down his life or fights for the country—both us became secessionist when the state seceded.

Christoph Rhodius

George Rlehwe[85] (duly sworn):

I am acquainted with the accused, I was assisting Schleicher in trying to raise a company for Sibley's Brigade, and I went recruiting to the house of accused, and spoke to the two sons of the accused and tried to get them to join the company and they refused. Witness then applied to the father to get him to use his influence with his sons to get them to join him. The substance of what the accused said was, when applied to, that it was near harvest time and the Indians being in the country it was inconvenient and impossible for the young men to leave the County then. I then called the attention of accused to the fact that a militia law would soon pass and their services might be required. He said, when that law passes, they would go and that he, accused, would use his influence with them to go.

George Rlehwe

Gustav Schleicher (duly sworn):

I am acquainted with the accused, have known him since he came to the country sometime in 1850 or 1851. I did not know him as well when he first came to county, but in later years I knew him much better. At one time my family stayed with him at his house for a month and at other time, and at other time I passed there frequently in getting to the country. I had frequent conversations with him on the subject of slavery. His views changed at different times. When he first came to the country, he believed that slavery was not a good thing for this country. I never at any time heard him condemn it as immoral or wrong. He had read that class of statistics and figures of Olmstead,[86] Helper, and others of similar views, and he had come to the conclusion that it, slavery, was not advantageous to the Southern Country. In later times about a year and a half ago, I rode above with him in a buggy on a considerable journey, and during that time I had many conversations with him, and he said to me that he had changed his views on the subject of slavery, and that he did not have now prejudices against the institution of slavery that he had when he first came here. He also on various occasions remarked to me that he regretted he had not the means to purchase negros—that he

73

and his family were forced to labor and he hoped some day to be able to buy a negro. Accused talked with me once as to the John Brown Raid and I remarked that it was the natural result of anti-slavery agitation to excite insurrections among the negros, and in reply he express in the strongest terms his disapprobation of any such schemes, and I think said he would go as for as any man in resisting them. The accused took little or no part in political matters, except in 1854, when he took part in what is called, or was called the Platform Meeting. He was disgusted with it, and in later years admitted it was folly, and I know that he scarcely went out of his house after in Election matters—I was candidate myself and know that he took little or part. I knew his (accused) two sons Hugo and Hillmar, I knew Hugo the best, they were known as great hunters. They were bold resolute young man, and very independent in spirit. The elder did not stay at home in later years so much. Hugo was once Clerk in a suttler's store at Fort Clark and once in a ranging company. The younger stayed at home more, but they both were absent a great deal. He was to a considerable extent dependent on them for support—they did not seem much to be under his control. They made money by hunting; my conclusion from facts under my eye is that their father did not have any great control over them—they came, and went as they pleased. I have seen but little of the accused since secession—he has lived a very retired life, and made no political exertions whatever—he was politically inactive. He was against secession, and ere against the formation, of the Southern Confederacy. He staid at home and was fond of talking and making pointed remarks, but I not believe he would do anything against the Govt., though he might talk—that is he would criticize the Government, and say that the secession movement was wrong, but I don't think he would take any action against the Government. I don't know as a matter of fact whether he is a dangerous or seditious person. I have seen but little of him since secession, and then I do not remember what conversation passed. Witness was shown the letter referred to by Slessinger and said it was directed to Col. Bernewitz and Ernst Brouneck— what follows the direction is a post script.

Gustav Schleicher

Emil Serger[87] (duly sworn):

I met the accused at Schleicher's Ranch and he said to me an order had been issued for all parties to come in and take the oath, and he advised witness to go in and take the oath, and also said he would notify others, so that no one might fail to take it through ignorance—he said that his sons were hunting and that he should find them and get them to come and take the oath if he could. A few days afterwards the accused came down with his son Hillmar and three or four others, and accused said that both his sons had agreed to take the oath— that Hillmar was with him for that purpose and Hugo had faithfully promised to do so, he said also that he had persuaded many others. The next day they took the oath. The first conversation above alluded to occurred sometime in July last. After taking the oath they promised him that they would remain at home, and further Hillmar had he had agreed to help his father reap some wheat for remaining at home, and as far as I know they remained at home.

Emil Serger

Gustav Freisleben[88] (duly sworn):

The letter referred to in the evidence of Buquor was here shown the witness and he said it was directed to Col. Von Bemewitz and Ernst Braunic—I knew both of those gentlemen and I knew them in Germany where they were living the last I knew of them. Col. Von Bemewitz is the brother-in-law of the accused, the other is not related but is an intimate friend. This letter is not addressed as is usual—the usual way in German is to address it at the beginning; letters are, however, sometimes addressed as this is. Some times letters are address at the beginning and sometimes at the end— many address their letters at the conclusion.

Gustav Freisleben

Charles Beseler[89] (duly sworn):

I am acquainted with the accused, and knew his two sons, and have known them for 10 or 12 years. I was at school with his two sons. I don't know of accused ever giving advice to any one as to conscription, but I heard in June last the accused in the presence of myself, my brother, and his two sons, talking very earnestly to them advising the to be quiet and stay at home and do their work, and not leave him to all the work. At another time early in July, I traveled in the road to Comfort with the accused [and] his two sons, and there we met cow hunters and we stopped, the boys commenced talking about the conscription law, the accused was in the midst of the and made a speech, and said to them stay at home and do their work, and said he heard that some of them were about the country, and did not like to comply with the conscription law, and he said while they were assembled together, he would give them a little advice. He told them to stay at home, to agree with the laws, and asked them if they did not see the danger that would come all over the country if they did not subdue themselves to the law, expecially *(sic)* the conscript law—this was a little while before martial law was declared, requiring the oath be taken—about 7 or 8 person, my brother and myself, accused two sons, Mr. Cramer and Mr. Bauer,[90] his brother-in-law and Mr. Tellgmann were there. I saw him, the accused, the 28th of July last, and he told me he had just come back from Comfort, and had hunted up his sons, and had persuaded them to take the oath the next day, my brother and his son Hillmar was with him—he said that the other men he met in Comfort were willing to take the oath and that they were all going to Boerne by his persuasion the next day to take the oath, and that his son Hugo had pledged himself to him that he would take the oath: two days after that both sons of the accused and my brother and six or eight more men, went to Boerne and took the oath on 30th July last.

Cross examined:

I am about 33—belong to no company. My brother I think went off with the two Degener boys, the party of 6 or 8 that I saw go in to take the oath I have not seen since, I think they are gone: the sons of the accused left on the 1st August 1862. The witness states that he was exempt from conscription by reason of his having a widowed mother without any other protector.

Charles Beseler

It is admitted by the accused that the person from whose body the letter was taken as stated by Lt. Lilly was a son of the accused.

Defense

Before entering at length upon the investigation of this case, it may be well to clearly understand the *nature, extent,* and *criminality* of the charge against the prisoner at the bar, that there may be no uncertainty or mistake, as to the accusation he is called upon to answer: after which, let us inquire whether the proof adduced substantiates the charge and shows the Defendant to have violated any civil, or military, law of the land, or that there is any cause, or even any *plausible* necessity to deprive him of his life, his liberty, or his property.

The Charge is in the following language, viz:

"That E. Degener is hostile to the Government of the Confederate States, and is a dangerous and seditious person and an enemy to the Government of the Confederate States."

As we understand the rules governing military Court, the accused is called upon to answer the charge—not the specifications—under which he must be condemned or acquitted. So far as the specifications and proof under them go to substantiate the charge, so far, only, can they be used to establish the guilt of the accused.

Every fact in the specification should be such, as, if proved would convict the prisoner of the charge, or at least might convict him, "If the facts stated in the specification, would not if proved, amount to the crime stated in the charge, both charge and specification must be rejected, for the court is pronounce only on the crime named in the charge, and on not other." American Military Laws Page 234. The first specification is to the effect that the Defendant has knowledge of a band of men who were coming themselves to fight here, and escape into Mexico of which he gave us information. If true, it would constitute no offense under any law, nor would it in any manner substantiate the charge. Hence it should be disregarded by the Court.

The second specification—which is that the Defendant in August 1862 by false seditious exaggerated and slanderous written statements, sought to bring the Confederate States Government into disrepute and array one class of the population in hostility to the other—if true, would constitute no crime, nor would it amount to the accusation named in the charge; and, if considered at all, should only be so far as the proof under it may to show that the Defendant is a dangerous and seditious person and an cnemy to the Confederate States Government. A like consideration can only be given to specification No. 3.

We apprehend no such offense, as is attempted to be set forth in the above charge, is known to the Constitution or law of the Confederate States or of any state thereof.

Such a charge is without authority or precedent in this country, save in the odious and unconstitutional Alien and Sedition laws of 1798 and '99 of which this would seem to be a counter part.

The Alien Act authorized the President to [order] all such alien as the might judge dangerous to the peace and safety of the United States or should have reasonable grounds to suspect were concerned in any treasonable or secret machinations against the United States Government to depart out of our territory—and in case of their refusal, on conviction to be imprisoned not exceeding three years. [91]

The Sedition Act made it a misdemeanor for a citizen to be engaged in seditious acts, or libelous and seditious writing against the U. S. Government.

It would almost seem that the charge is this was drawn under those acts, so similar is their language: yet they were virtually dead letter from the time of their passage, and at the succeeding Congress, being deemed in violation of the plainest provisions of the Constitution and subversive of the dearest rights of the people, were swept from the statute books; and none such disgrace the laws of our State or infant Confederate.

Our law makers, the officers of our Government, and our military commanders could not have desired the creation of any such crime, or the punishment of our citizens under any such charge, or they would have long since so declared.

If the necessity to arraign our citizens under such charges exist to day, so much the more did it exist during the previous to the last session of our Congress.

To be hostile to the Confederate States Government is no crime: to be a dangerous and seditious person and an enemy of the Confederate Government is no crime: The Defendant might be all, or either, and yet be guilty of no crime.

If, however, it be true that the Defendant is a seditious and dangerous person and hostile, or an enemy, to the Confederate Government, in times of war like these, when required for the general good and safety of all, he may be a proper subject Martial Law, as *"lex necessitates,"* so far as to place him under such obligations restraints as shall deter, or prevent, him from doing any injury to our Government or our cause.

Pass here the question as to the legality of this Court and its want of jurisdiction, and taking it for granted that cases coming under this charge are within its *peculiar province*, it seems there is but one question presented for our consideration, by which to determine the guilt or innocence of the Defendant, viz: *Is the Defendant a seditious and dangerous person, and hostile, or an enemy, to the Confederate Government?*

The only facts, we apprehend, upon which the Government relies are in substance as follows, viz:

The two sons of the Defendant, Hugo and Hillmar, between the ages of 21 and 24, while seeking to avoid conscription by attempting to make their escape into Mexico with 67 other armed men, were killed in a fight with Confederate troops on the 10th of August 1862 near Fort Clark in this State.

That the letter, dated August 1st 1862, and addressed to Col. Von Bernewitz and Braunschweiger and Counsel Ernst Bramigk at Coethen in Germany, one the brother-in-law and the other an intimate friend of the Defendant, which was found upon the body of one of Defendant said sons, was written by Defendant.

That in a conversation, while under arrest, as to the death and conduct of Defendant sons in the fight, he stated that he know his sons would not surrender; that they were right and the Confederate States troops were right, as each were fighting for opinions sake; and that he knew all the men, meaning the so styled '*bushwackers*'; that there were the best shots in the country and that the Confederate States troops could not have whipped then if they had not the advantage.

We cannot believe that any of the testimony on the part of Government—excepting the letter, can be deemed of sufficient importance to require a moment's serious consideration of this court. If there is any other testimony in this case, tending in any manner, to establish charge or to show any acts of disloyalty or enmity to the Government we have been unable to discover it. Hence we shall confine ourselves mainly to the Letter in reviewing the Government's evidence.

It will no doubt be contended that the letter shows two facts—
1st the Defendant is hostile in his feeling to our Government:
2nd that he had knowledge of, or was connected with, a band
of men opposed to our Government and who were about to
leave the County to avoid conscription.

The letter—supposing the same to have been written by a
resident or a citizen of the Confederate State, taken by itself,
without any surrounding circumstance, might admit of such a
construction, but not so, if written by a stranger. It is but a
laconic recital of facts to parties in a foreign and friendly
Country, and may will have been written by a friend of the
Confederate Government, when excited and depressed at the
thought of the near and perhaps final departure to a distant
country of two sons upon whom he had depended for support
in his declining years, and when deprived, as a consequence of
a war of which there were few signs of an termination, of
many of the necessaries of life, and [when] poverty and want,
if not starvation, seemed to stare him in the face.

The following are the principal facts recited in the letter:
"That as yet the war has kept distant from Texas, thought not
its inconveniences; that martial law is in force; those from 18
to 35 [are] ordered to the field, and those from 35 to 50 drilled
as militia; the union young men were in the mountains to
avoid Conscription, and the Confederate troops hunt them;
that there is danger of Civil or Vendee war—to avoid which
unionist retreat across the Rio Grande; Martial law to the
utmost rigor; those who suspect their names as being on the
black list conceal themselves and have every thing ready for
flight; the crops a failure; provisions, clothing and powder

very high in price, and scarce; severe draught; the people of the South madly abuse the United States Government and are ready to make a desperate fight for their rights of slavery; that according to the newspapers we have killed more enemies that the North has inhabitants; what will be the end, those at a distance perhaps can better judge, though his judgment is unchanged; Provost Marshals have the power to treat the suspected at discretion; the Southern troops threaten to take no more prisoners; if the south remains successful it may happen the Germans will have to emigrate again; the Southerners have great hatred against the 'Dutch,' all of them are suspected as being Black Republicans, that is enemies of slavery: the Southerners are provoked at the idea of Siegel and his Missouri Germans gaining victories, as all the Americans think themselves born Generals; from the effects of the blockade no shingles, nails, or glass to be had in San Antonio; the departure—meaning across Rio Grande—of Defendants boys resolved upon the day previous to the writing of the letter; their horses saddled, pack animal ready, to be joined by 47 other select men; one more dinner—then farewell perhaps never to see his sons again; not a cent of money in the pockets, as Confederate money among Indians and Mexican robber-bands is worth no more than in Mexico; Mama is baking the last bread for a long, long time for her beloved boys."

Without any knowledge of the writer excepting his identify, and leaving out such portions of the letter as shown his relation to any of the persons therein referred to, of what crime, simply upon that letter, could he be found guilty?

Russell or any other newspaper scribbler might have written the same without being the enemy of the country.

Are not the facts therein stated mainly correct? It is true some of them are over drawn and there is a vein of sarcasm running thought much of the letter. Is it not true that there is almost a failure of crops in Western Texas, that provisions, clothing, and all the necessaries of life are very dear? Is it not true that there exists a strong prejudice among the Americans of the South against the Germans, especially of Western Texas? It is useless to deny the fact, though we need not now inquire the cause or whether the same is well or erroneously founded.

But in justice to the Defendant, and to give a fair and impartial construction to the Letter, we must consider its surrounding circumstances.

The Defendant, is a native of Germany, fifty odd years of age; has resided in Texas since 1850; has a small farm upon the frontier, from the cultivation of which, and the manufacture of shingles by the labor of himself and his two sons Hugo and Hillmar, he has obtained his support; this year he has made no crops; could not have known of the intended departure of his sons until the day previous, as on the 30th of July they took the oath of allegiance at his persuasion, and just previous to that time they had promised to remain quietly at home with him. He wrote the letter on the day of the departure of his sons, evidently under much excitement, as they acting contrary to his repeated advice, and fearing that he might never see them again. Under those circumstances the Defendant writes a letter of his brother-in-law and an old friend in Germany. Is it a wonder that his heart was heavy and his words despondent? Yet he does not say aught against the Confederate Government or its institutions.

The only portion of the letter which should really an explanation is that which might seem to indicate that he had some knowledge of a party of young Germans and who to avoid conscription and a Vendee war were going to Mexico. It cannot be gathered from the letter that Defendant sons or those by whom they were to be jointed had any other object than to keep from being conscripted and any collision with Confederate troops by escaping into Mexico. Being determined not to be conscripted, they were going out of the country to avoid a Vendie *(sic)* war, such as laid waster *(sic)* and deluged in blood the blood the district of *La Vendie* in France in the revolution of 1793 when conscription was attempted to be enforced there.

The simple knowledge of that fact however, with any connection with the parties or their conspiracy could not make the Defendant guilty of any crime, or answerable to any law. Will it be said that because a father failed to report that his sons were fleeing the country that, therefore, he must punished? There are few elder Brutuses of to day so unselfishly patriotic or with hearts so callous as to order the execution of their own sons.

The letter must appear to have been written furtherance of the Conspiracy—not as a mere relation of facts, or as the speculative opinions of the party—in order to fasten guild upon him. De Hart 350-51 Ros. Crim. Laws 85 & 86.

We might rest our case here, as we believe the testimony on the part of the Government, utterly fails to establish the charge or to show any cause for the farther detention of the prisoner. It does not show that he is a dangerous person, or that he was ever committed any seditious or unfriendly acts towards the Government.

Believing the Defendant wholly innocent of the charge preferred against him, and that he might clear himself of every suspicion of disloyalty, or hostility to the Government we assumed the initiative and, as we conceive, have fully shown his fidelity to the Confederate Government.

We have shown by the uncontrodicted *(sic)* testimony of four witness who have known the Defendant for twelve years, since his residence in Texas, most of the time quite intimately that, though prejudiced against the institution of slavery upon his emigration here during the last few years his views and feelings have undergone an entire change upon that subject, and that he is now in favor of slavery and would become the owner of Negros had he the means.

Upon hearing that the North designed arming the slaves to fight against the South he expressed an earnest determination, if that was done, to take up arms and fight against the North of the bitter end of the War.

We have shown also by the testimony of four witnesses that the Defendant not had nothing to do with any parties in opposing, or in evading the laws, civil or military, of the Confederate government, but that he used every effort to persuade his unfortunate sons, as well as all other in his vicinity who were opposed to the Government, to abide by the Confederate laws and submit quietly to all of the military regulations. Time after time, at home, with his sons, and wherever he might chance to meet any unfriendly to the Confederate Government, we find him advising and urging a submission to the laws. He urged upon his sons the necessity of taking the oath of allegiance and of enrolling their names under the Conscript Act. We find him at all time complying with the laws and martial regulations; and at no time do we find his acting, talking or plotting against the Government.

We know of no act of treason, or sedition, or of hostility against the Confederate Government of which the Defendant is guilty. We know of no civil or military law, of no martial rule or regulation, or no order of any General or of any subaltern which he has violated. He is not hostile to the Confederate Government because he has been shown to be friendly to it; he is not a dangerous or seditious person, because he has been shown to have exerted his utmost influence to cause a peaceful submission to, and a full compliance with, our laws, and to prevent strife, civil war and blood-shed among our own citizens.

And yet, is it possible that the Defendant may be condemned by this Court? If so, under what name? We look in vain through the catalogue of civil, military, or political offences to characterize it. From an intimation casually thrown out by the Judge Advocate, during the trial, per chance of the Defendant may be accused of *neutrality*, the nature, culpability, origin, or application, of that crime we are unable to determine.

We know of but one pretended crime a king to it in the history of civilized nation, the crime of *incivism, or want of patriotism*, which sprang from the blood brains of the Jacobin Club.

If we are to be tried for such a *Mysterious* and *undefined*, we would ask the poor privilege which was extended by the Revolutionary Tribunal of France, of being tried by a jury of *Sousculottes* [*Sanscoulottes*].

But could the crime of *neutrality* be applied to an old man beyond the age of conscription, nearly "three score years," living upon the frontier in an Indian County, which barely the means of support, who has fully complied with all of the laws and requirements of the Government, because to forsooth he has not voluntarily shoulders his musket and gone forth to peril his life in the defense of his adopted County?

We cannot believe such an accusation can seriously engage the consideration of this Court for moment. The evidence, however, controverts that "*far fetched*" accusation.

The Defendants life, at first of bright promise, has been checkered by adversity and bitter misfortunes, having experienced the horrors and sufferings to two Revolutions the calamities of the third one now falling heavily upon him, and if, in the judgment of the more zealous, he has not in the Revolution reached the highest standard of loyalty and patriotism, as by the evidence adduced, he stands before this Court guiltless of the charge, let the veil of charity be drawn over his "short-coming" and let that elevated kindness and generosity, which has this far marked the course of the South in this war, characterize the conduct of this court in it deliberations and judgments.

A severer penalty than can possibly be inflicted by this court has already fallen upon the unfortunate old man, in the untimely death of his misguided sons.

Waelder & Upson of
Counsel for Defendant

It shall be my purpose briefly to respond to the Defense of the accused—

The 1st Specification, seems to be sustained by the evidence. It proved that "a band of men hostile to the Confederate Government, in Kerr and other counties were organized, that in August 1862, to fight here and escape into Mexico." Can this be denied? It is further proved, that the accused had knowledge of this band, that he wrote a letter to them, that he went once in five miles of their camp and conversed with their leader, and that he saw his two sons and Tellgmann start out to join them—

Can it then be contended that he had no knowledge of the conspiracy? It must be that he had knowledge, and it is clear that he withheld that knowledge from the authorities. Had he, as a good citizen ought to have known, informed the proper authorities, instead of writing letters and holding commerce with these parties, he would have perhaps saved the lives of his sons, and saved the Confederacy some of her son, who died in that fight.

But the counsel says that to *know* of such a conspiracy and to conceal that the fact is no crime—He is mistaken. Whoever conceals any felony is guilty of a crime.

Russell in crimes Vol. 1-pa 45—says, speaking on this subject, "Generally mispresions *(sic)* of felony is taken for a *concealment of felony* and to observe the commission of a felony without using an endeavors to apprehend the offender, is a Mispresion *(sic)*, a man being bound to discover the crime of another, to a magistrate, with all possible expedition."

This specification to whence the counsel did not pay even the *cold* respect of a passing glance, seems to be well substantiated.

The counsel did not copy this specification fully in his defense and it may be he did not clearly see or overlooked import.

With regard to specification 2nd, which was based on the Letter in evidence, it may be sufficient to say a few works. That the letter contains many false slanders and exaggerated statement is plain; but in as much it was written to foreigner and not to our own citizens it may be disregarded? I know no laws prohibiting a man from slandering to foreigners the house of his adoption. The charge was proved under the impression that the letter in question was addressed to one of our citizens; the original translation had no direction to it and the Judge Advocate was misled.

The 3rd specification, the counsel has misunderstood. The first of it is that the accused aided and assisted in arming and fitting out certain enemies, and surely this is a crime. It has

91

nothing to with the Alien and Sedition Laws, upon which the counsel had discussed. If is prohibited by the laws of our and in this state by express proclamation. Did he not aid, assist in getting out young Tellgmann and his two sons? His letter shows that they started from his house, that he know they would join 47 picked men, that his wife prepared their provisions and can be doubted that he did to this extent assist them.

The object of this examination is under the *charge*[?] to test the political states of the accused: Is he or not an enemy to our Government? His best friend say they regarded him but as neutral—He told Edwards that his sons were right and that Edward was right. If he believed his sons and the others right, ought he not, would he not, did he not aid them?

Again his letter, which is evidently written under great excitement and without disguise and is in truth a glorious, transcript from the writers very heart, shows what his sentiments are: it is full of bitter sarcasm, even against our government and cause. He believed that if the South conquered, he would have to emigrate and believing this, is it likely that he would be an enemy to such a Government?

Who can read the letter and not feel that he head and heart that conceived it, is not alive to our great struggle for liberty and life.—Fortunately for our country, we have but a few such citizens and with little power to do wrong.

C. S. West
Judge Advocate

Confederate States vs. Eduard Degener

October 2, 1862

In the above cause the Judge Advocate submits his reply to the defense of the accused: And thereupon the Court being cleared for deliberations, after due consideration found as follows:

Of the 1st Specification—Guilty.
Of the 2nd Specification—Not Guilty.
Of the 3rd Specification—Guilty of holding correspondence with the enemies of the Confederate States, but the correspondence not treasonable in its character; of the remaining portion of specification 3—Not Guilty.

Of the Charge we find him hostile to the Government of the Confederate States, an enemy to the same, and not guilty as the remaining portion of the charge. And the Commission do sentence the said Eduard Degener: *To enter into a Bond, with two good securities to be approved by the President of this Commission, in the sum of Five Thousand Dollars, conditioned that he shall conduct himself during the War as a good and loyal citizen to the Confederate States.*

October 2, 1862 - Case No. 36
Confederate States[92] vs. Ferdinand Simon[93]

The accused Ferdinand Simon being brought before the Commission and having introduced Malcolm G. Anderson Esquire as his counsel and announcing himself ready to hear the Charge and Specifications against him the same were read aloud to him by Judge Advocate as follows:

Charge

That Ferdinand Simon has acted as an enemy to the Confederate States and is a dangerous person to be at large and levied war against the Confederate States.

Specification 1st
 In this that in the State of Texas and in the month of August 1862, or in the later part of July of the same year, the said Simon was in arms in opposition to the Confederate States, and in concert with its open enemies—all this near Ft. Clark in this State at the date above specified.

Specification 2nd
 That said Simon did, near Ft. Clark in the State of Texas in the month of July or August 1862, aid by his countenance and presence, and by active participation with arms, certain traitors who were gathered together at the above stated time and place, and that said aid and active armed assistance was given said parties in a fight between them and certain Confederate soldiers under Lt. McRae, said Simon being one of said band, and firing there on the Confederate Troops.

Specification 3rd
That said Simon did in the months of July and August 1862 attempt secretly and covertly and in violation of laws of the Country and the orders of the Military Commanders, attempt to leave the country.

Signed C. S. West
Judge Advocate

To which the accused Ferdinand Simon pleaded *"Not guilty,"* and thereupon announced himself ready for trial: when the examination of witness on the part of the Government was began and continued until the Commission adjoined till to morrow morning October 3rd at 8:30 o'clock. A.M.

* * *

Office Military Commission
San Antonio, October 3rd 1862

The Commission met pursuant to adjournment.
Present:
 Major Charles Russell President
 Captain B. F. Neal C.A.P.A.C.S.
 John C. Howard, Esquire
 C. Upson Judge Advocate and Recorder

Confederate States[94] Case No. 36 vs. F. Simon
The examination of witnesses in this cause, this day continued and the Commission adjourned until to morrow morning at 9:00 o'clock A.M.

C. Upson,
Judg. Ad. & Rec.

* * *

October 4, 1862

Frank Radoz being duly sworn entered upon his duties as clerk of this Commission.

Confederate States - Case No. 36 vs. F. Simon

In this cause the witnesses of the accused were duly sworn and examined and further examination postponed by reason of the absence of other witness.

* * *

October 8, 1862

Confederate States – Case 36 vs. F. Simon

In this cause the examination of witnesses was resumed and continued until to morrow morning at 9;00 o'clock.

C. Upson, Judge Advocate and Recorder

* * *

October 9, 1862

Confederate States - Case No. 36 vs. F. Simon

The testimony in this cause was this day concluded and the counsel for the accused asked until 4 P.M. to finish his defense; whereupon the court adjourned until 4 o'clock P.M. of this day at which time a full commission having convened in pursuance of adjournment, the counsel for the accused read and submitted to the Commission his written defense for the accused.

There the Commission adjourned until tomorrow at 10:00 o'clock A.M., to which time the Judge Advocate was allowed to submit his reply

C. Upson, Judge Advocate and Recorder

* * *

October 10, 1862

Confederate States Case No. 36 vs. Ferdinand Simon

The reply of the Judge Advocate to the defense of the accused having been submitted, and all of the evidence and statements in this cause being before the Commission, the Commission cleared for deliberation, and having duly considered thereof, the Commission find the accused Ferdinand Simon as follows:

Of the first Specification—Guilty
Of the second Specification—Guilty
Of the third Specification—Guilty
Of the Charge—Guilty

And the Commission do therefore sentence the said Ferdinand Simon to be hanged by the neck until dead—at such time, and place as the Commanding General appoint.

ENDNOTES

01. "Records of the Confederate Military Commission in San Antonio, July 2—October, 1861" Edited by Alwyn Barr in 'Southwestern Historical Quarterly', Volume LXXI, No. 2, October 1967 252-253.

02. A detachment from Captain James Duff's Company of Partisan Rangers arrested Joseph Krust in early June 1862 for Unionist activities. He was held in the Bexar Jail until his hearing on July 17, 1862. He operated a hotel in Castroville. Krust was born about 1817 in France. The date he arrived in Texas is not known. Krust married Catharina Burger on October 27, 1852 in Medina County. They were the parents of at least two children. Krust was a member of Company C, Medina Independent Battalion, 31st Brigade District. He was elected a county commissioner during the war. His date and location of death is not known.

03. "Records of the Confederate Military Commission in San Antonio, July 2—October, 1861" Edited by Alwyn Barr in 'Southwestern Historical Quarterly', Volume LXXI, No. 2, October 1967 253.

04. A detachment from Captain James Duff's Company of Partisan Rangers arrested Leonhard Petterich in Castroville in early June 1862 for Unionist activities. He was also held in the Bexar County Jail until his hearing on July 17, 1862. Petterich was a master saddler. He was born about 1826 in Bavaria. The date he arrived in Texas is not known. Petterich married Catherine Haldy on July 19, 1858 in Medina County. Catherine Haldy Petterich died in November 1860 in Castroville. Petterich was a member of Company C, Medina Independent Battalion, 31st Brigade District in early 1862. On October 12, he enrolled in Haby's Company. After the war Petterich moved to San Antonio.

'

05. Samuel Gallitzen Newton was born on March 27, 1823 in the Cherokee Indian Nation. By the 1850s the family was living in Dallas County. On February 20, 1854 Newton married Mary Elizabeth Tompkins in Bexar County. They were the parents of eleven children. Newton was a lawyer and organized the Bexar Guards in the summer of 1861 and was elected captain. On May 7, 1862 the company became Company H, 3rd Regiment Texas Infantry. By the end of the war he was a lieutenant colonel. Samuel G. Newton died on June 21, 1874 at San Antonio.

06. "Records of the Confederate Military Commission in San Antonio, July 2—October, 1861" Edited by Alwyn Barr in 'Southwestern Historical Quarterly', Volume LXXI, No. 2, October 1967 253-258.

07. Julius Schlickum was a Kendall County Moderate [a Gray] Unionist. He was not a member of the Union Loyal League. Schlickum was born about 1825 in Prussia. He arrived in Texas on the *Franziska* from Munster in 1846. Schlickum returned to Prussia and on September 27, 1849 he married Caroline Therese Klier. They were the parents of three children. Schlickum was one of the secretaries of the 1854 German San Antonio Convention. He urged the Convention to be careful and not go to the extreme in the affairs of Texans. He was elected a Kendall Justice of the Peace in early 1862 and was elected captain of Company B [Kendall County], 3rd Regiment 31st Brigade District in the spring of 1862 and was in the process of being elected a lieutenant colonel of the regiment in June 1862. Schlickum "tried with all my power to reason and convince the leaders of this group [Union Loyal Group] to reconsider this foolish attempt. I repeatedly depicted to them the ruin of the settlement. In vain!" After martial law was declared Captain Duff arrested him in June 1862. He was sentenced to prison for the remainder of the war. He along with Philip Braubach and Friedrich William Doebbler escaped on July 19, 1862 and went to Mexico. He made arrangements for his wife and children to join him in Matamoras. When Theresa and her three children arrived in 1863

Endnotes

they learned Schlickum had died of yellow fever. She and her children returned to Munster.

08. Erastus Reed was a merchant at Boerne. He was born on April 1, 1826 in Georgia. By 1860 he was living near Boerne in what is now Kendall County. On September 7, 1863 he married Almira L. Toby in Bexar County. They were the parents of five children. Erastus Reed died on February 2, 1882 in Bexar County.

09. J. Rudolph Radeleff was a Gillespie County Unionist and likely an original member of the Union Loyal League. He was born about 1829 in either Holstein or Denmark. The date Radeleff arrived in Texas is not known, but by October 1859 he applied for U. S. Citizenship. He was in partnership with John and James Hunter to provide beef for the U. S. Army frontier posts. The Gillespie Rifles condemned him in March 1862 for his Unionist activities. He was arrested by Captain James Duff in early June 1862 at San Antonio. The Confederate Military Commission convicted Radeleff of Unionist activities. He was ordered banished from the Confederacy. After the war Radeleff returned to Gillespie County and received his U. S. Citizenship on January 6, 1868. He was elected the Presiding Justice [County Judge] of Gillespie County and reelected in 1872. J. Rudolph Radeleff died in Gillespie County, likely by 1880.

10. Friedrich Wilhelm Doebbler was a Gillespie County Unionist. He was both a Forty-Eighter and Freethinker. Doebbler married Henriette [maiden name not known] about 1849. They were the parents of at least five children. Doebbler had to flee 'Germany' about 1851 and settled in Gillespie County. He was a Gillespie Merchant: likely an original member of the Union Loyal League; condemned by the Gillespie Rifles in March 1862 for Unionist activities; and wrote several articles for Northern Newspapers critical of the Confederacy. Captain James Duff arrested him in early June 1862 and he was

convicted by the Confederate Military Commission for disloyalty. He escaped and fled to Mexico were he waited out the war. He returned to Gillespie County after the war. Friedrich Wilhelm Doebbler died about 1915 in Gillespie County.

11. This statement credited to Schlickum is very much correct. There were about 100 insurgents hiding 'in the wood' and Schlickum did not belong to the Union Loyal League.

12. Again Schlickum is correct. There was a Unionist organization in Bexar County. According to Colonel Henry McCulloch, who was commander of the military district of San Antonio, in his letter of March 28, 1862 to Governor Lubbock the "Germans in one quarter of this city [San Antonio] have organized a company of 73 men well armed with shot guns, rifles and pistols and plenty of ammunition."

13. Judge Jonathan Hampton Scott was the Chief Justice in Kerr County. Scott was born in 1803 in Miller's Run, Washington County, Pennsylvania. The family arrived in Texas on August 20, 1830 and settled in Brazoria. Scott married Nancy Miden on November 12, 1833 in Brazoria. They were the parents of three children. Scott joined the Texian Army on June 23, 1836. Mary Miden Scott died about 1843. He married Diana Brown, the daughter of the founder of Kerrville about 1845. They were the parents of nine children. The family arrived in present day Kerr County about 1855. On March 26, 1856 Scott was elected Kerr Chief Justice and served until 1862. He was a strong secessionist. Toward the end of the war Scott moved his family to Gonzales. Jonathan Scott died February 27, 1874 in Gonzales County.

14. Johannes Holzapfel was a close friend of Julius Schlickum. He was born about 1802 in Germany. Holzapfel married Anna Martha Schmidt. Their marriage date is not known, nor is the number of children they were the parents of. The family arrived in Texas in 1844

Endnotes

and settled in Comal County. Holzapfel's name is on the 1846 Republic of Texas Tax Roll living in Comal County. The family arrived in the Comfort area in 1854. After Schlickum was arrested he assisted Therese and the Schlickum children. Holzapfel's date and location of death is not known.

15. George Wilkins Kendall was a prominent Kendall County sheep rancher. He was born on August 22, 1809 at Mount Vernon, Amherst, New Hampshire. He was an early printer. About 1833 he moved to New Orleans and founded the *New Orleans Picayune*. In 1841 he joined the Texian Santa Fe expedition and was captured by Mexican forces. He was released in May 1842 and in 1844 published *Narrative of the Santa Fe Expedition*. He served with Benjamin McCulloch's Ranger Company during the Mexican War. After several years travelling in Europe Kendall married Adeline de Valcourt in 1849. They were the parents of four children. In the early 1850s he established sheep ranching in what is now Kendall County. George Wilkins Kendall died on October 21, 1867 in Kendall County.

16. Joseph Graham was the Kendall Chief Justice and the county's provost marshal. He was born about 1811 in Ohio. About 1849 he moved to Argentina where he married an unknown woman. They were the parents of two children. His wife died about 1855 and Graham and his children returned to the United States on the ship *American* on December 15, 1856 and settled in the Texas Hill Country. He married Ellen Moore on May 20, 1861 in Bexar County. They were the parents of two children. Joseph Graham fled Texas about 1863, but returned by 1865. Joseph Graham died on October 4, 1867 in Kendall County.

17. Seaman Field was the first sergeant in Duff's Company of Parisian Rangers and living in the area before the War. He was born about 1829 in Ohio. He arrived in the area by 1860. Field enlisted in Duff's Company on May 4, 1862 and was elected first sergeant. He was

elected first lieutenant in Duff's Company B on October 16, 1862 and promoted to captain on February 7, 1863. Field resigned on November 6, 1863 due to disability. He married about 1865. The name of his wife is not known, nor is the exact date and location of marriage known. They were the parents of at least three children. His wife died by 1880, likely in Kaufman County, Texas. Seaman Field married Achash Abbot in 1881, likely in Kaufman County. They were the parents of at least one child. Seaman Field died about 1905, likely in Grant County, New Mexico.

18. "Records of the Confederate Military Commission in San Antonio, July 2—October, 1861" Edited by Alwyn Barr in 'Southwestern Historical Quarterly', Volume LXXI, No. 2, October 1967 253-256.

19. Valentine Frederick Haass was a Castroville merchant arrested by a detachment from Duff's Partisan's Rangers in early June 1862 for Unionists activities. He was born on April 3, 1829 in Bavaria. He arrived in Texas on the *Montague* from New York in August 1850. He was a member of Company D, Medina County Independent Battalion, 31st Brigade District, Texas State Troops in the spring of 1862. Haass married Alka Gerdes on August 13, 1863 in Medina County. They were the parents of three children. Valentine Haass died on September 10, 1907 at Castroville in Medina County.

20. Valentine Frederick Haass enrolled in Company H, 3rd Regiment Texas Infantry on July 19, 1862.

21. "Records of the Confederate Military Commission in San Antonio, July 2—October, 1861" Edited by Alwyn Barr in 'Southwestern Historical Quarterly', Volume LXXI, No. 2, October 1967 260-272

22. Philip Braubach was the Gillespie County Sheriff and captain of a home guard company that was Unionist. He was born on July 28, 1829 in Wiesbaden, Duchy of Nassau. Braubach arrived in Texas on

the *Neptune* from Wiesbaden in 1850 and by the mid-1850s was living in Gillespie County. He was both a Forty-Eighter and Freethinker. Braubach was elected Gillespie County sheriff in August 1860. In February 1861 he organized a home guard company that was in service until February 1862. Braubach was the first lieutenant in Kuechler's December 1861 Company. Captain Duff arrested Braubach in June 1862 and he was tried and convicted of Unionist activities. He was sentenced to prison for the remainder of the war upon which time he was to be expelled from the Confederacy. He escaped and fled to Mexico where he organized a guerrilla company that operated along the Rio Grande. On May 4, 1864 he joined the First Regiment [Union] Texas Cavalry. Braubach was mustered out of Union service on October 31, 1865 at San Antonio. He married Louise Schutze, the daughter of Louis Schutze, another Gillespie County Unionist. They were the parents of at least seven children. Philip Braubach died on June 30, 1888 in San Antonio.

23. Michael Vollmer was born about 1814 in Bavaria. The date he arrived in Texas is not known. He married Henriette [maiden name not known] about 1851, location of marriage not known, but it was likely in Texas. They were the parents of five children. Michael Vollmer died about 1864, likely in Gillespie County.

24. Jacob Kuechler was an original member of the Union Loyal League and a Gillespie County insurgent. He was born about 1823 in Hesse-Darmstadt. Kuechler was a member of *Die Vierziger* [The Forty] a university fraternity of socialists who arrived in Texas in 1847 on the *St Pauli* sponsored by the *Adelsverein*, a German immigration company. They established the short lived-Bettina Colony on the Llano River. Kuechler moved to Gillespie County in the mid-1850s and became a surveyor. He married Mary Petri on May 31, 1856 in Gillespie County. They were the parents of at least three children. In December 1862 he was appointed to raise a company for the Frontier Regiment. However, he enrolled only Unionists and the governor

disbanded the company. In the spring of 1862 he was elected captain of Company E, 2nd Regiment [Gillespie County], 31st Brigade District. Kuechler was the captain of the Gillespie Company of the league's military battalion. He commanded this company in the August fleeing insurgent group. He survived the Nueces Battle and returned to Gillespie County. In October 1862 he led another insurgent group fleeing to Mexico. The Confederates overtook them on the Rio Grande and many were killed. Kuechler remained in Mexico until the end of the war. After the war he was elected Texas General Land Office Commissioner. Kuechler died on April 4, 1893.

25. Friedrich Wilhelm Doebbler was a merchant in Fredericksburg. He was born on March 25, 1824 in Luckenwalde, near Berlin, Prussia. He took part in the German Revolution in 1848 and was also a Freethinker. He married Henriette Hanzog in 1848, likely in Prussia. They were the parents of six children. Doebbler and his brother, Louis, and his family fled Prussia in 1851 and settled in Gillespie County. He obtained his U. S. citizenship on September 24, 1857 in Gillespie County. Doebbler was an original member of the Union Loyal League. He wrote several newspaper articles critical of the Confederacy which were published in northern papers. He was condemned by the Gillespie Rifles in March 1862. Captain Duff arrested him in June 1862 for unionist activities and he was tried by the Confederate Military Commission and found guilty of 'disloyalty'. He and Julius Schlickum and one other man escaped and made their way to Mexico where he waited out the war. He returned to Gillespie and became a New Dealer. Friedrich Wilhelm Doebbler died on December 23, 1913 in Gillespie County.

26. Frank Van der Stucken was the commander of Company C, of Taylor's Battalion of Texas Cavalry. It was raised in Gillespie County. Van der Stucken was born about 1831 in Belgium. He arrived in Texas in 1846 with Henry Castro, the founder of Castroville. Van der Stucken married Sophie Schoenewolf on December 23, 1852 in Gillespie County. They were the parents of five children. Van der

Stucken was a member of the Gillespie County Rifles and helped draw up the resolution condemning the Unionists. He raised a Confederate company in May 1862. When Taylor's Battalion was consolidated with Yeager's Battalion and became the 1st Regiment Texas Cavalry his company became Company E. In August 1864 Van der Stucken was elected the Gillespie County Chief Justice. In the spring of 1865 Van der Stucken was forced to flee back to Belgium to avoid Unionists' reprisals.

27. Very little is known about Hilmar Von Gersdorff. He apparently was living in Gillespie County in 1862. Van Gersdorff was born about 1827 in 'Germany'. The date he arrived in Texas is not known. He married Johanna Frydeck. The date and location of their marriage is not known. Van Gersdorff died in September 1870 in San Antonio.

28. Charles Henry Nimitz was a hotel owner in Fredericksburg. He was born on November 8, 1826 in Bremen. He arrived in Texas in 1846 and was one of the first settlers at Fredericksburg. Nimitz married Sophie Dorethea Muller on April 8, 1848 in Gillespie County. They were the parents of twelve children. He organized The Gillespie Rifles in June 1862. Nimitz was the Confederate enrollment officer for Gillespie County. Charles Henry Nimitz died on April 28, 1911 in Gillespie County.

29. The Hunter brothers were Fredericksburg merchants. The two that settled in Fredericksburg were John M. Hunter and James M. Hunter. They had been in business with Philip Braubach providing beef to the frontier military post.

30. Gustav Schleicher was a prominent member of the Texas German community. Schleicher lived in San Antonio. Schleicher was born on November 19, 1823 in Hessen-Darmstadt. He graduated from the Darmstadt Gymnasium and studied engineering and architecture at the University of Giessen. He was a member of *Die Vierziger* [The Forty] a university fraternity of socialists who arrived in Texas on the *St*

Pauli sponsored by the *Adelsverein*, a German immigration company. The Forty established the short-lived Bettina Colony. Schleicher married Elizabeth Tinsley Howard in 1856 in San Antonio. They were the parents of at least eight children. Schleicher was a member of the Fifth Texas Legislature from 1853 to 1854 and a member of the Texas Senate from 1859 to 1861. During the war he served as a Confederate engineering officer. After the war Schleicher served as a member of the Forty-Fourth and Forty-Sixth U. S. Congress. He died in office on January 10, 1879 in Washington, D. C. Schleicher County is named in his honor.

31. James M. Hunter was born in December 1829 in Buncombe County, North Carolina. He arrived in Texas in 1851. He married Philippine Keller on August 9, 1860 in Gillespie County. They were the parents of eleven children. On March 4, 1862 he enrolled in Davis' Company, of the Frontier Regiment and was elected first lieutenant, but served most of the time as the regiment's quartermaster. In February 1863 he was promoted to captain and placed in command of Company A. He remained in command for a year. In mid-1864 he was promoted to major and placed in command of the Third Frontier District headquartered in Fredericksburg. By late 1864 Hunter was relieved of command. Hunter moved to Mason County where in December 1862 he was elected Justice of the Peace in Precinct No. 1. In 1870 he was appointed a Ranger captain. In 1878 he was elected a member of the Texas House of Representatives and served from April, 1878 to August 21, 1878. In November 1878 Hunter was elected Mason County Chief Justice. In 1883 he and his family moved to Edwards County and helped organized the county and was selected the first county judge in 1890. James M. Hunter died on August 31, 1907.

32. George Weinheimer was a Gillespie County farmer. He was a Unionist. Weinheimer was born on September 19, 1824 in Prussia. The family arrived in Texas on the *Strabo* in 1845 and settled in Gillespie County. George Weinheimer married Laura Elenora Dapperich on September 8, 1851 in Gillespie County. They were the

parents of ten children. Weinheimer was a member of Braubach's home guard company from February 1861 until February 1862. He was a member of the Gillespie company of the league's military battalion. Weinheimer was a member of Schuetze's Company of the Third Frontier District in January 1864. Many members of this company were pro-Union bushwhackers. After Louis Schutze was hanged in February 1862, Weinheimer was a member of Krauskopf's Company of the Third Frontier District in May 1864. George Weinheimer died on January 22, 1912 in Gillespie County.

33. Frederick Fresenius was a Fredericksburg merchant. He was born about 1826 in Prussia. The date Fresenius arrived in Texas is not known. He married Bertha Basse, the daughter of Pastor Henry Basse' on November 28, 1855 in Gillespie County. They were the parents of only one child. Fresenius was a member of the Gillespie Rifles in February 1862 and took the Confederate oath of allegiance the same day. Frederick Fresenius died about 1875 in Gillespie County.

34. Engelbert Krauskopf was a gunsmith in Fredericksburg. He was born on August 21, 1820 in Prussia. Krauskopf arrived in Texas on the *Andacia* in 1846. He married Rose Herbst on January 28, 1849 in Comal County. They were the parents of seven children. Krauskopf was a second lieutenant in the Gillespie Rifles. After Louis Schutze was hanged he reorganized the company in May 1864 and remained its captain until the end of the war. Engelbert Krauskopf died on July 11, 1881 in Gillespie County.

35. Henry Stephen Wilhelm Basse was the first Protestant pastor for Fredericksburg. He was born on October 9, 1804 in Thuringia, Prussia. Pastor Basse married Fredericke Charlotte Quintel on November 29, 1832 in Elsoff, Prussia. They were the parents of nine children. The family arrived in Texas on October 23, 1846 on the *York*. He served as the Protestant pastor for three years when he became a merchant in November 1849. Pastor Stephen Wilhelm Basse

died on January 10, 1865 at Fredericksburg. It is interesting to look and study his testimony. It was very neutral, neither supporting nor condemning Braubach despite the fact Braubach was responsible for beating Basse's son Oscar in May 1862.

36. Charles Schwarz appears to have been an early Unionist, but by mid-1862 no longer supported them. He was born about 1839 in Waltenhein Bavaria. The family arrived in New Orleans on the *Henry Grinnell* in February 1855 and came on to Texas. Charles Schwarz married Elise Behrens about 1859, location of marriage not known. They were the parents of at least seven children. In 1860 he was a mail rider. He was a member of Kuechler's December 1861 Company and by February 1862 was a member of the Gillespie Rifles. Sheriff Philip Braubach arrested him in May 1862 when he attempted to enroll in Captain Van der Stucken's Company C, Taylor's 8th Battalion Texas Cavalry. Captain Van der Stucken paid his fine and Schwarz returned to his company. He remained with the unit when it became Company E, 1st Regiment Texas Cavalry and served until the end of the war and received a parole at San Antonio on September 16, 1865. Charles Schwarz died about 1875, likely in Gillespie County.

37. Wilhelm Victor Keidel was the medical doctor at Fredericksburg. He was born in March 1825 at Hildesheim, Hanover. Keidel received his medical degree from the Georg Augustus University at Goettingen, Hanover in August 1845. He arrived in Texas on the *Margarete* in December 1845. When the Mexican War started Keidel enlisted in a Texas military unit for six months. When he was released from the service he moved to Gillespie County. In the first Gillespie County election Keidel was elected chief justice. He moved to the Live Oak community and helped organize the cultural-political club. He treated many of the colonists without charge. He married Albertina Mary Kramer about 1849, location of marriage is not known. They were the parents of one son, who was born on July 1, 1852 and Albertina died on the same day. On October 16, 1856 Dr. Keidel married Caroline

'Lina' Kott at Fredericksburg. They were the parents of one son who was born on August 14, 1865 and Lina died the same day from fever. Keidel was a member of the Gillespie Rifles. Dr. Wilhelm Victor Keidel died of typhus pneumonia on January 9, 1870 in Fredericksburg.

38. Ottocar Mueller was the postmaster and druggist in Fredericksburg. He was born about 1814 in Prussia. He married Elise [maiden name not known] about 1846, likely in Prussia. They were the parents of at least four children. The family arrived in Texas on the *Soenburg* in 1850 and settled in Fredericksburg. Mueller was a member of Schuetze's November 1863 company. Many members of this unit were pro-Union bushwhackers. After Schuetze was hanged in February 1864 Mueller became a member of Locke's Company of the Third Frontier District. Ottocar Mueller died about 1875 in Gillespie County.

39. Friedrich Wilhelm von Wrede, Jr. was an early member of the *Adelsverein* and merchant in Fredericksburg. He was born on December 31, 1820 in Hessia. The family first arrived in Texas in 1836. They arrived at New Orleans on the *Manko* on January 5, 1836. Wrede's mother died of yellow fever in December 1837. Wrede and his father travelled to East Texas, St. Louis, and New York. They returned to Germany in 1843. In 1844 Wrede was appointed secretary to Prince Carl of Solms-Braunfels and arrived with him in Texas. Wrede remained in Texas after Prince Solms returned to Germany. From 1851 until 1859 he was the Gillespie County clerk. In 1859 he was elected to the Eighth Texas House of Representatives from November 7, 1859 until April 1861. He married Sophie Bonzano about 1850, location of marriage is not known. They were the parents of five children. Due to his pro-secessionists views Wrede and his family returned to Wiesbaden in 1865. He remained there until 1871. No further data.

40. John Adam Schuesslar was a Gillespie County farmer. He was born on August 24, 1811 in Bonfeld, Württemberg. He married Eva Katherine Dieschinger on January 13, 1835 in Württemberg. They were the parents of nine children. The family arrived in Texas on the *Dyle* in 1846 and settled north of Fredericksburg at a place they named Cherry Springs. Adam Schuesslar died on April 7, 1884 in Mason County.

41. Joseph Petsch [Poetsch] was very likely a member of the August insurgent group. He was born on November 4, 1838 in Nassau. The family arrived in Texas on the *Washington* in 1845 from Frickhofen. Petsch was a member of the Luckenbach Bushwhackers. After the Nueces Battle he returned to Gillespie where he hid for the remainder of the war. Petsch married Anna Maria Weinheimer on November 21, 1865 in Gillespie County. They were the parents of at least seven children. Joseph Petsch died in Gillespie County on December 24, 1917.

42. Oscar Basse was the son of Pastor Henry S. W. Basse. The family arrived in Texas on the *York* in 1846. Basse enrolled in the Gillespie Rifles in February 1862 and took the Confederate oath of allegiance on the same date. He enrolled in Davis' Company of the Frontier Regiment in March 1862 and in May was beaten by the Unionist at Doebbler's Bee Hall because he enrolled in Davis's Company. He served with the company until the expiration of his term of service in February 1863. On February 11, 1867 he married Mathilda Pape in Gillespie County. They were the parents of at least seven children. Oscar Basse died on February 12, 1914 in Bexar County.

43. August Siemering was a Gillespie County Unionist and likely an original member of the Union Loyal League. He was born on February 8, 1828 [1830] in Brandenburg, Prussia. He was both a Freethinker and Forty-Eighter. He arrived in Texas on the *Republic* from Hahlhausen, Prussia in 1851. He first settled in Comal County where on May 29, 1852 he married Emma Boehme who arrived in

Endnotes

Texas on the same ship. It does not appear they had any children. Siemering was a major participate in the 1854 German Convention in San Antonio. Emma Boehme Siemering either died or they were divorced as on June 12, 1859 Siemering married Clara Schuetze, the daughter of another Gillespie Unionist. They were the parents of eight children. Siemering was a member of Kuechler's December 1861 Company. In May 1862 he enrolled in Van der Stucken's Company C, Taylor's 8th Battalion Texas Cavalry where he was elected junior second lieutenant. He resigned his commission on March 4, 1864 and returned to private life. Siemering was appointed the Gillespie County Chief Justice in 1865. Siemering later established the German language *Freie Presse fuer Texas*. August Siemering died on September 19, 1883 in San Antonio.

44. Joseph Walker was a Travis County citizen who was a strong secessionist. He was born about 1815 in Ohio. Walker arrived in Texas in the late 1840s and settled in Travis County. He married Ann [maiden name not known] Cloud a widow. They appear to have had no children. In 1853 Walker and a partner purchased the *Texas State Times*, which they renamed the *Austin State Times*. In 1857 Walker purchased in interest in the *Texas State Gazette*. After Governor Lubbock dismissed Kuechler's Company in early 1862 he appointed Walker to raise a new company. Walker did so and on February 25, 1862 at Fort Martin Scott he enrolled the new company which was named Davis' Company A, The Frontier Regiment. Joseph Walker died on August 3, 1886 at Austin in Travis County.

45. William Wahrmund Sr. was the Gillespie County Chief Justice. He was born on April 31, 1824 in Wiesbaden, Nassau. Wahrmund married Amalie Schildknecht shortly before arriving in Texas. They were the parents of ten children. William Wahrmund was one of four brothers who arrived in Texas on the *Talisman* from Wiesbaden in 1846. The brothers all settled in Gillespie County. William Wahrmund Sr. was elected Gillespie Chief Justice in 1852 and served until August 18, 1862. He was a member of the Gillespie Rifles and took

the Confederate oath of allegiance in February 1862. Wahrmund was the first lieutenant of Locke's Company of the Third Frontier District in January 1864. After Locke deserted and joined the Union Army Wahrmund was elected captain and served until the end of the war. He was elected Gillespie County Chief Justice several more times. He died on June 20, 1890 while serving as Gillespie County Chief Justice.

46. "Records of the Confederate Military Commission in San Antonio, July 2—October, 1861" Edited by Alwyn Barr in 'Southwestern Historical Quarterly', Volume LXXI, No. 2, October 1967, 258-260.

47. Heinrich Frederick Lochte, Sr., the individual who refused to sell Duff corn for Confederate paper money in June 1862 and a Gillespie County Unionist. Lochte was born on October 17, 1809 in Peine, Hanover. He married Dorothy Moellering about 1835, likely in Hanover. They were the parents of at least five children. The family arrived in Texas on the *Herkules* in November 1845 and settled in Gillespie County where Lochte became a merchant. After his refusal to sell corn for Confederate paper Duff arrested him for depreciation of Confederate money which was a violation of martial law. Heinrich Frederick Lochte, Sr. died on July 19, 1867 in Gillespie County.

48. Johann Friedrich Dambach was born on May 22, 1808 in Widdern Baden-Württemberg. He married Ludovicke Pfeifer on October 8, 1834 in Widden. They were the parents of eight children. It appears Dambach first arrived in Texas in 1845 and by 1846 had returned to Germany. The family arrived in Texas on the *Weser* in 1854. After the war Dambach was forced to return to Widdern because of his testimony against the Unionist. He died on December 9, 1879 in Baden-Württemberg.

49. Karl Ludwig Frederick Dambach was the son of Johann Friedrich Dambach above. He was born on November 2, 1837 in Widdern, Baden-Württemberg. He arrived with his father on the *Weser* in 1854,

114

Endnotes

and settled in Gillespie County. Ludwig Dambach married Johanne Jane Hahn on April 17, 1860 in Gillespie County. They were the parents of two children. Dambach enrolled in Van der Stucken's Company C, Taylor's 8th Battalion Texas Cavalry in May 1862. He remained with the unit when it became Company E, 1st Regiment Texas Cavalry and served until the end of the war. Dambach died on February 16, 1894 in Gillespie County.

50. James P. Waldrip was born about 1827 in Alabama. He married Wincy M. [maiden name not known] about 1848, likely in Coosa County, Alabama. They were the parents of seven children. The family arrived in Texas about 1853 and settled in western Gillespie County. Waldrip organized a 'squad' for the Third Frontier District in January 1864. Waldrip is identified as the alleged leader of the *Haengerbande* [hanging gang]. He was responsible for some of the deaths blamed on James Duff. Waldrip was indicted for the murders of John Blank and William Feller. Henry Langerhans shot and killed Waldrip at the Nimitz Hotel in March 1867.

51. "Records of the Confederate Military Commission in San Antonio, July 2—October, 1861" Edited by Alwyn Barr in 'Southwestern Historical Quarterly', Volume LXXI, No. 2, October 1967 272-277.

52. Johann Peter Ulrich was a San Antonio carpenter. He was born on November 14, 1828 in Bavaria. He married Christina M. [maiden name not known] about 1853, likely in Bavaria. They were the parents of at least five children. Ulrich arrived in Texas in 1854 on either the *Weser* or *Hampden* and settled in Bexar County. He obtained his U. S. citizenship in August 1860. Johann Peter Ulrich died on January 17, 1890 in Bexar County.

53. John M. Hunter was the oldest of the Hunter brothers of Gillespie County. He was born on September 2, 1821 in Tennessee. Hunter arrived in Texas in the late 1840s. He married Sophie Ahrens on

March 9, 1848 in Gillespie County. They had no children. John M. Hunter died on September 5, 1870 in Gillespie County.

54. "Records of the Confederate Military Commission in San Antonio, July 2—October, 1861" Edited by Alwyn Barr in 'Southwestern Historical Quarterly', Volume LXXIII, No. 1, July 1969 83.

55. Henry Joseph Richarz was a prominent Medina County citizen. He was born on September 8, 1823 in Prussia. Richarz married Josepha Schaufhausen about 1847 in Prussia. They were the parents of at least nine children. Richarz was a Forty-Eighter who had to flee Germany. He first went to New Orleans in 1850 and on to Texas that same year. Richarz was a D'Hanis farmer and postmaster. He was elected captain of Medina Precinct 3 home guard company and later major and commander of the Medina County Independence Battalion of the 31st Brigade District. Members of Duff's Company arrested him in early June 1862 for Unionist activities. Upon his release Richarz was immediately elected Medina Chief Justice. He was later a Ranger captain. Henry Joseph Richarz died on May 21, 1910 at D'Hanis in Medina County.

56. "Records of the Confederate Military Commission in San Antonio, July 2—October, 1861" Edited by Alwyn Barr in 'Southwestern Historical Quarterly', Volume LXXI, No. 2, October 1967 277.

57. A detachment from Duff's Company arrested Blasins Kieffer in early June 1862 for Unionist activities. He was born about 1835 in Alsace. The date he arrived in Texas is not known, but it was likely after 1850. Kieffer married Adeline Halberdier on January 12, 1859 in Medina County. They were the parents of six children. Kieffer was a member of the Medina Knights of the Golden Circle in 1861. After his release from jail he was elected a Medina County Commissioner in August 1862. The Medina 1867 list of voters shows he was driven out of the county because he was a good Union man. Adeline Halberdier Kieffer

died about 1866 in Medina County. Blasins Kieffer married Louisa Schule on February 25, 1870 in Medina County. They were the parents of four children. Blasins Kieffer died about 1879 in Medina County.

58. "Records of the Confederate Military Commission in San Antonio, July 2—October, 1861" Edited by Alwyn Barr in 'Southwestern Historical Quarterly', Volume LXXI, No. 2, October 1967 277

59. Francis Joseph Wipff was arrested by a detachment from Duff's Company in June 1862 for Unionist activities. He was born on February 19, 1820 in Alsace. Wipff arrived in Texas in late 1846 and settled at D'Hanis in Medina County. In 1855 he married Maria Anna Derier at D'Hanis. They were the parents of ten children. Wipff was a member of Company A Medina Independence Battalion, 31st Brigade District in early 1862. Francis Joseph Wipff died on March 21, 1900 at D'Hanis.

60. "Records of the Confederate Military Commission in San Antonio, July 2—October, 1861" Edited by Alwyn Barr in 'Southwestern Historical Quarterly', Volume LXXIII, No. 2, October 1969 246 - 268

61. Eduard Degener was the head of the Union Loyal League. He was born on October 20, 1809 in Brunswick. Degener married Maria Bernewitz about 1830 in Brunswick. They were the parents of four children. Degener was a Freethinker and a Forty-Eighter. He was a member of German National Assembly at Frankfurt in 1848. When the 1848 Revolution failed Degener was forced to flee and arrived in Texas in the latter part of 1848 and settled at Sisterdale. He was a member of the Sisterdale *Der Freier Verein* in 1853. He was a member of national *Freier Maenner/Freimaennerverein* in 1853. He was a major speaker at the German 1854 Convention at San Antonio. Degener conspired with Frederick Law Olmsted in the 'Deep Water Plan' to separate West Texas and make it a free state. In late August

1862 Confederates arrested Degener and charged him with being 'hostile' to the Confederate Government. After the war he moved to San Antonio and opened a wholesale grocery business. He was a member of the Texas Constitution Conventions of 1866 and 1868. He was a major supporter of the plan to split Texas into five states, one of which would be controlled by the Germany community. Degener was elected to the U. S. Congress and served from March 1870 to March 1871. Eduard Degener died on September 11, 1890 at San Antonio.

62. Colin Dickson McRae was the officer in command of the Confederate pursuit force and resulting Nueces Battle. He was born on September 22, 1835 near Clarksville in Red River County, Texas. McRae enrolled in Donelson's Company K, 2nd Regiment Texas Mounted Rifles in February 1861. He was elected first lieutenant. In late July 1862 Company K, was part of a three-company task force sent to Fredericksburg to destroy the insurgency. On August 3, 1862 Captain Donelson dispatched McRae with 94 men to overtake the fleeing insurgent group. At 3:00 a.m. on August 10, 1862 they attacked the camp. The insurgency lost nineteen men killed at or near the battle site. McRae lost 2 men killed, and 4 who would die from their wounds and 15 other wounded. On October 1, 1862 McRae married Margaret D. Haw at San Antonio. They were the parents of one child, a son. On the same day he was promoted to captain. He took part in the Galveston Battle on January 1, 1863. McRae's son died on June 9, 1864. Captain Colin Dickson McRae died on September 10, 1864 from typhoid fever.

63. Very little is known about Edward Slessinger. He was living in San Antonio by December 1860. Slessinger was the 2nd Sergeant in the November 1, 1862 Minute Man Home Guard Company of Captain Asa Mitchell. No further data.

64. Pasquale Leo Buquor was a south Bexar County farmer. He was born in July 1821 in Louisiana. He married Maria De Jesus in 1841 in

Louisiana. They were the parents of at least five children. The family arrived in Texas by 1848 and settled in southern Bexar County. On November 29, 1860 he was elected first lieutenant of the Alamo Rifles. In May 1861 Buquor enrolled in Company A, 3rd Regiment Texas Infantry and was elected its captain. His company was the first permanent garrison at Camp Verde. He remained with the company until the end of the war. P.L. Buquor died on March 15, 1901 in Wilson County.

65. Von Bernewitz was Degener's father-in-law.

66. Ernst Bramigk was a very close family friend.

67. B. is Degener's daughter, Bertha, born about 1836 in Brunswick. She married Christian Rhodius on March 15, 1854 in Comal County. The 'charming little daughter' was Mary, who was born in 1862.

68. It is interesting that Degener, who was head of the Union Loyal League, used the term guerrilla warfare to describe acts of members of the League's military arm.

69. It is also of special interest to note that Degener described the conditions as 'Civil War is on the eve of breaking out.' Most writers claim that the League members that were hiding in the mountains were just trying to avoid the war and had not desire to take part in the fighting. All Unionists accounts made by members of the fleeing group stated they were going to Mexico where they would go on and join the Union Army.

70. This Degener comment shows the despair many of the Unionists were feeling and the real possibility of a Southern victory and the impact it would have on them.

71. Franz Siegel was a Missouri Freethinker and Forty-Eighter and the leader of the Missouri German community. He organized the Missouri Home Guards that kept Missouri in the Union. Siegel was appointed a Union major general in command of a corps that was having great success in the east.

72. This sentence provides a great deal of information. First it tells about how many pack animals the fleeing group had; one for every 3 men. Second it confirms that not all the Unionist met at one place. There was a second group of about 47 men located someplace other than the assemble area at Turtle Creek. This was at a base camp located on the headwaters of the South Fork of the Guadalupe River.

73. William J. Edwards was a member of Duff's Company. He was born on May 12, 1840 in Choctaw County, Mississippi. The date he arrived in Texas is not known. By 1850 Edwards was living in Comal County. He enrolled in Duff's Company on May 4, 1862 at San Antonio. Edwards remained with the company until the end of the war. On May 12, 1869 he married Josephine Walters in Bexar County. They were the parents of eleven children. He likely died in Bexar County about 1915.

74. Dr. Ernst Kapp was a Sisterdale Freethinker and Forty-Eighter. He was born on October 15, 1808 in Ludwigshafer, Oberfranken. Dr. Kapp received his Ph.D. from the University of Bonn in 1828. He married Ida Kappel about 1830 in Germany. They were the parents of at least five children. The family arrived in Texas on the *Franziska* in 1849. Dr. Kapp was the president of the Sisterdale *Der freie Verein;* it appears he changed from a radical to a moderate and even purchased a female slave about 1857. Because of lack of support for the Unionists he was forced to return to Germany in 1865 where he died at Dusseldorf on January 30, 1896.

75. Dr. Charles Ganahl was a Kerr County medical doctor. He was born in 1824 in Augusta, Georgia. Dr. Ganahl married Virginia Mctaggart

Jordan Wright in 1854 near Tallahassee, Florida. They were the parents of three children. Dr. Ganahl became ill with tuberculosis and in 1858 moved to Texas and settled about halfway between Kerrville and Comfort. The community that grew up around his home and office became known as Zanzenberg. Dr. Ganahl was elected the Kerr County delegate to the secession convention in 1861. During the war he served as chief surgeon on General Slaughter's staff. After the war he refused to take the oath of allegiance to the United States and moved to Mexico where he remained for several years. He eventually returned to Texas and opened his medical office at Galveston. Dr. Charles Ganahl died in 1883 at his home in Kerr County.

76. On May 14–15 in 1854 the Texas Freethinkers and Forty-Eighters organized a German Convention to be held after the *Staats-Saengerfest* (State Singers Festival) in San Antonio to unite the various German communities into a political force. The Texas *Der freie Verein* (The Free Society) a branch of the nation *Freier Mann Verein* (Freeman's Association) sponsored the convention. Among other things the convention did was to declare was an evil and that abolition was the business of the state. This convention lead to the Texan Anglos belief that the Texas Germans were abolitionist.

77. Ernest Hermann Altgelt was the founder of Comfort. He was born on July 17, 1832 at Düsseldorf, Prussia. Altgelt arrived in Texas in 1852 by way of New Orleans. He arrived in the Comfort area in 1853. On Jul 23, 1855 he married Emma Murck in Bexar County. They were the parents of at least nine children. Altgelt was a secessionist and due to this he returned to Prussia until the war was over. After he returned to Texas in 1865 he opened a law practice. Ernest Hermann Altgelt died on March 28, 1878 at his ranch about 25 miles north of San Antonio.

78. Hugo Degener was a son of Eduard Degener and a Kendall insurgent. He was born about 1842, likely in Brunswick. The family arrived in Texas 1852 and settled in Sisterdale. Hugo was a second lieutenant in

Kuechler's December 1861 Company and a lieutenant in the Kendall County of the league's military battalion. He fled with the August insurgent group and was killed at the battle site.

79. Moritz Weiss was a Kendall County insurgent. He was born about 1836 in Prussia. The date the family arrived in Texas is not known. By 1855 they were living in the Comfort area. Weiss was a member of the Luckenbach Bushwhackers and a member of the Kendall Company of the league's military battalion. He fled with the August insurgent group but survived the Nueces Battle and returned to Comfort. In October 1862 Weiss fled with the second insurgent group and he was killed at the Rio Grande on October 18, 1862.

80. Altgelt here is referring to the March meeting at Bear Creek where the league's military battalion was organized.

81. Ernest Cramer was the captain of the Kendall Company of the league's military battalion. He was born on May 23, 1836 in Schweinfurt, Bavaria. Cramer first arrived in Texas in 1853 and worked as a merchant. He was the first lieutenant in John W. Sansom's 1859 Ranger Company. He returned to Bavaria and arrived back in Texas on the *Iris* in 1860. On September 12, 1861 Cramer married Charlotte Apollon Bauer in Kerr County. They were the parents of six children. Cramer was a member of Harbour's February 1861 Kerr Home Guard Company. He was likely an original member of the Union Loyal League. He was in the August 1862 fleeing insurgent group and survivor of the battle. He returned to the Hill County but by early fall had fled to Mexico where he waited out the war. In the early 1870s he moved his family first to California and than to Idaho where he died on July 10, 1916.

82. William Tellgmann was a Kendall County insurgent. He was born about 1831 in Brunswick. He and his brother, Charles, arrived in Texas 1852. They were Freethinkers and Forty-Eighters. Charles joined the Confederate Army while William refused. He was a

member of Kuechler's December 1861 Company and a member of the Kendall Company of the league's military battalion. He fled with the August 1862 insurgent group and was seriously wounded at the Nueces Battle. Tellgmann was one of the wounded insurgents executed.

83. Heinrich Joseph Schwethelm was a Kendall County insurgent. He was born on September 4, 1840 in Prussia. The family arrived in Texas about 1850 and in the Comfort area in 1854. Schwethelm was a member of several ranger companies before the war. He was a corporal in Harbour's February 1861 Home Guard Company. Schwethelm married Emilia Stieler on March 19, 1862 in D' Hanis. They were the parents of three children. Schwethelm was a member of the Kendall Company of the league's military battalion. He fled with the August 1862 insurgent group, survived the Nueces Battle and fled on to Mexico where he made his way to New Orleans and enrolled in Company A, First Regiment [Union] Texas Cavalry. He deserted his company after the Las Rucias Battle on June 24, 1864 above Brownsville. Henry Joseph Schwethelm died on August 16, 1924 in Kerr County.

84. Christoph Rhodius was the son-in-law of Eduard Degener. He was born about 1830 in Prussia. Rhodius was likely a Freethinker. He arrived in Texas on the *Dyle* in 1846 and first settled in Guadalupe County. Rhodius married Bertha Degener on March 15, 1854 in Comal County. They were the parents of at least two children. Rhodius was very likely a member of the Kendall Company of the league's military battalion. He enrolled in Jones' Company of the Third Frontier District on March 21, 1862. Rhodius' date and location of death are not known, but it appears he is buried in Bexar County.

85. No information on George Rlehwe was located.

86. Frederick Law Olmsted was born on April 26, 1822 at Hartford, Connecticut Charlotte Law Hull and John Olmsted were his parents.

Poor health, especially his eyes kept him from attending Yale. In 1843 Frederick hired on the ship *Ronaldson* bound for China. When he returned he wrote an account of his travels titled *A Voice From The Sea*. About this time Olmsted was becoming an abolitionist and decreased his interest in the organized church. Frederick and his younger brother, John who was quite sickly, travelled to England and Europe and Frederick published a book *Walks and Talks of an American Farmer in England* which did quite well. Frederick met and made friends with several leading Abolitionists such as William Lloyd Garrison, Henry Ward Beecher, and his sister Harriet Beecher Stowe. In 1853 the two Olmstead brothers made a trip through the eastern slave states which resulted in the book *A Journey in the Seaboard Slave States* which was well received. Later that year the two brothers decided to visit Texas and learn about slavery there. He was not impressed with the Texans, but did find the German immigrants doing quite well with free labor. They found among the German immigrants a group of Freethinkers and survivors of the 1848 Germany Revolution now called Forty-Eighters. He became very good friends with the German-Texas Radicals such as Adolph Douai, the *San Antonio Zeitung* editor, Edward Degener and Charles N. Riotte, Sisterdale Radicals. These Freethinkers and Forty-Eighters were already looking for a way to establish a free state of West Texas [now the Texas Hill Country]. They conceived a plan, sometimes called the "Deep Water Plan" because it ran through deep water and demanded all their navigation skill. At this time proslavery and antislavery forces were contending for Kansas. Olmsted had contacts with abolitionist groups, such as the New England Emigrant Aid Company of Boston, who sent immigrants and supplies into Kansas. "Why not do something similar in Texas?" Some of the zealous Kansas free-soilers were already saying they would "take Western Texas next"; pointing out the method Maine used to have gained her independence from Massachusetts and became a free state in 1820. They pointed out that the western Texas area included a large number of Germans and Mexicans and very few slaveholders. Friedrich Kapp, a Forty-Eighter and Abolitionist who was also a nephew of Sisterdale's Ernst Kapp, urged his northern readers to consider making their homes in western Texas. Based on voting records of August 1853, Douai informed northern abolitionist that there were sufficient numbers in west Texas to vote for a free state. He pointed out that of 50,000 Anglos living in the area; some 10,000 were born north of the Mason-Dixon Line. Added to these 10,000 there were another 11,000 Germans and other Europeans and 25,000 Mexicans that could be persuaded to vote for a free West Texas. These Freethinkers and Forty-Eighters conducted a state wide convention of Germans in San Antonio in 1854. The Texas Anglos learn of part of the plan and a 'fire storm" forced them to down play the idea. Therefore, little came of this plan, but it did plant in the minds of Texas Freethinkers and Forty-Eighters the idea of a free West Texas. Frederick Olmsted married his brother's widow, Mary, in 1859. They were the parents of four children. Frederick Olmsted and Calvert Vaux set about designing what became New York's Central Park. It opened to the public in December 1859 and by 1865 was drawing more than seven million visitors. Frederick Law Olmsted died on August 28, 1903 at the McLean Hospital at Waverly, Massachusetts.

87. Emil Serger was a Kendall County carpenter. He was born on March 27, 1831 in Prussia. Serger arrived in Texas about 1854 and in the Comfort area about 1856. Serger took the oath of allegiance to the Confederacy on September 30, 1861 at Comfort. He was in the group that recovered the insurgent bodies in August 1866. Serger married Marie Sittel about 1864, location of marriage not known. They were the parents of at least four children. Emil Serger died on June 25, 1900 in Kendall County.

88. Gustav Freisleben was the San Antonio City surveyor. He was born about 1818 in Anhalt-Dessau. Freisleben arrived in New York on August 7, 1854. The date he arrived in Texas is not known, but on December 14, 1854 he applied for U. S. Citizenship which he received on November 3, 1858. No further data.

89. Charles Philip Beseler was a Kendall County Unionist. He was born on September 4, 1840 in Wesel, Prussia. The family arrived in Texas on the *Franziska* in 1848. His brother William was a member of the August 1862 fleeing insurgent group and killed at the battle site. He married Minna Maetz on December 25, 1862 in Kendall County. They were the parents of at least six children. Beseler was a member of Company C, 3rd Regiment of the 31st Brigade District. He was very likely a member of the Kendall County Company of the league's military battalion. Beseler enrolled in Duff's Company E on January 4, 1863. His Confederate service records show him at home sick in March 1864 and on April 21, 1864 as a deserter. Beseler fled Texas and on February 14, 1864 enrolled in Company C, First Regiment [Union] Texas Cavalry and appointed a sergeant. He received his discharge on June 17, 1865. Charles Philip Beseler died on April 10, 1908 in Kendall County.

90. Leopold Bauer was a member of the August fleeing insurgent group and the first man killed in the battle. He was born about 1839 in Prussia. The family arrived in Texas about 1853 and in the Comfort area in 1854. Bauer was a member of the Kendall Company of the league's military battalion.

91. This statement by Eduard Degener's attorney is very interesting. The myth has grown up that the insurgent group was travelling under some type of proclamation issued by the Texas Governor or some Confederate authority. Exhaustive research results turns up no evidence that such a proclamation was ever issued. What was issued was President Davis' Proclamation of August 14, 1861 giving anyone living in the Confederate State boundaries 40 days to take the oath of allegiance or leave the country. Here Degener's attorney is admitting that Davis's Proclamation was the only one given.

92. "Records of the Confederate Military Commission in San Antonio, July 2—October, 1861" Edited by Alwyn Barr in 'Southwestern

Endnotes

Historical Quarterly', Volume LXXIII, No. 2, October 1969 270 –
272.

93. Ferdinand Simon was a member of August fleeing insurgent group
    and was wounded at the Nueces Battle. He was born about 1826 in
    Hesse-Darmstadt. It is believed Simon arrived in Texas on the *Strabo*
    from Darmstadt in 1845 and settled in Comal County. He married
    Caroline Bauer on September 1, 1856 in Kerr County. They were the
    parents of at least four children. Simon took the oath of allegiance to
    the Confederacy on May 27, 1861. He was a member of the Kendall
    Company of the league's military battalion. Simon fled with the
    August insurgents and was wounded in the Nueces Battle. He escaped
    from the battle site, but was captured by a Confederate scout about
    four days after the battle. The Confederate Military Commission
    found Simon guilty of acting as an enemy of the Confederacy and
    ordered him hanged. But, before the sentence could be carried out the
    Confederate Government declared martial law was annulled. Simon
    was transferred to Austin for trial.

94. It is not clear what the trial outcome was, but it appears he spent the
    remainder of the war in jail. Ferdinand Simon died in July 1878 at his
    home near Boerne.

95. The Court Recorder changed before Simon's trial, and the new one's
    records were very sparse.